Selections from

THE THOUGHTS

Crofts Classics

GENERAL EDITORS

Samuel H. Beer, *Harvard University*

O. B. Hardison, Jr., *The Folger Shakespeare Library*

BLAISE PASCAL

Selections from

The Thoughts

TRANSLATED AND EDITED BY

Arthur H. Beattie

THE UNIVERSITY OF ARIZONA

Harlan Davidson, Inc.
Arlington Heights, Illinois 60004

PRINTED IN THE UNITED STATES OF AMERICA

82   83   84   85   86CB12   11   10   9   8

CONTENTS

INTRODUCTION

The name of Blaise Pascal is intimately associated with the Jansenist Abbey of Port-Royal, and rightly so. Yet Pascal could affirm, during the persecution of the Jansenists, that he was not *of* Port-Royal. However close his ties with the movement, whose spokesman he became during the controversy with the Jesuits, it is nonetheless true that Pascal's inquiring mind, always seeking the truth in the midst of contradictions, could never rest within the confines of any system or any school. Jansenism influenced Pascal, especially in reinforcing his notion of the primordial importance of original sin and of grace in any effort to understand the essentially double nature of man; Pascal, in his turn, greatly influenced the Jansenist movement of Port-Royal. But to Pascal one cannot properly attach any label that would tend to situate him within a doctrine or school less broad than the Christianity of the Roman Catholic Church.

Briefly, Jansenism, which draws its name from Bishop Jansenius of Ypres in Belgium, author of a commentary on the teachings of Augustine on grace, was a rather puritanical movement within the Roman Catholic Church. Its doctrines of salvation through grace bear a strong resemblance to Calvin's teachings on the same subject. As in Calvinism, the basic notion of man's total depravity and utter worthlessness, coupled with the idea of salvation of the elect through grace, led to a severe discipline and a strict moral code on the part of its adherents. This severity brought the Jansenists into conflict with the Jesuits whom they accused of laxity and of using specious casuistry in their eager attempts to win and hold converts to the faith.

The Jesuits and Jansenists were rivals, too, in their pedagogical endeavors. Of course there was no rivalry in terms
of numbers, for the Society of Jesus, as the leading body
of educators of Europe, carried on its teaching activities in
many fine schools; the educational work of the Jansenists
in France was centered primarily at Port-Royal. Their
school there was one of unusual thoroughness and excellence. The tragic poet Jean Racine received at Port-Royal
the education that permitted him to know so intimately
the plays of Aeschylus, Sophocles, and Euripides. It is
proper to see in his *Phaedra*, as in the *Thoughts* of Pascal,
a reflection of Jansenist teachings concerning original sin.
Phaedra, who has been described as a Greek with a Jansenist conscience, is an example of the hopeless depravity
of humanity when divine grace is withheld.

Pascal's sister Jacqueline took orders as a religious of the
convent of Port-Royal. Pascal himself was, however, a lay-
man. He visited the institution on occasion and spent periods in one of the guest houses where austere men found
a refuge for contemplation and for serious spiritual dis-
cussions with their fellows. He is one of the glories of
Port-Royal, yet never totally and precisely of Port-Royal.

The fascination of Pascal's *Thoughts* sometimes leads
the casual reader to overlook the importance of the author's
work in mathematics and science. His intuitive mathematical genius had been revealed in quite early childhood, a
revelation that led his father to present to him a copy of
Euclid for light leisure-time reading. If Pascal did not
develop the infinitesimal calculus, it is perhaps because his
unquenchable curiosity led him constantly to turn to new
ventures before he had fully explored the consequences of
his brilliant discoveries. He furnished the foundation upon
which Leibniz was to build the calculus. His studies on
conic sections and on laws of probability are far from
insignificant.

In physics, Descartes and Pascal clashed over the question of atmospheric pressure and the vacuum. Descartes
argued from first principles and was wrong; much more

modern in his approach, Pascal conducted experiments, carefully measuring the height of a column of mercury at the base and at the summit of a high tower in Paris and of a steep and lofty volcanic peak in Auvergne; his conclusions helped lay the groundwork for numerous subsequent scientific and technological developments.

In the immediate background of the *Thoughts* are the eighteen *Provincial Letters* through which Pascal defended the Jansenists and mercilessly attacked the Jesuits. Urbane, witty, sly, devastating (and unfair in the exaggeration and in the use of quotations out of context that regularly characterize such writings), the *Provincial Letters* are masterpieces of polemic literature.

But Pascal is, and always will be, first and foremost the author of the *Thoughts*. These are the numerous fragments he had written for eventual incorporation in a work he planned to compose in defense of the Christian religion. At his death, he left them assembled in bundles, having effected a rough, tentative grouping by bringing together in these various packets passages bearing some relationship of one theme to another.

It must be borne in mind that Pascal died at the age of thirty-nine. There is in everything he wrote a youthful enthusiasm, a juvenile joy of discovery, a fascinating juggling with ideas and with words. The conventional rhetoric of his day made great use of contrasts, but Pascal's rhetoric spurns the academic principles of the schools. Pascal finds in himself, in life, and in the universe a host of contradictions, of seemingly irreconcilable and incomprehensible oppositions. The truth lies not in accepting one term and rejecting the other, not in seeking a middle ground, but in accepting both. Thus in this lively, vivacious style, varying in tone from sublime majesty to petty triviality, is a reflection of Pascal's concept of the all-embracing nature of truth. He startles us with sudden images of terror; he shocks us by throwing light into dark recesses of our subconscious; he elevates us with illuminating flashes of mystic ecstasy; he plays so skillfully upon our senses and our imagination that we wait breathlessly for the solution he will propose, for we cannot longer endure the dilemma in which he involves us so desperately. He opens abysses beneath our feet and the gates of heaven above our heads in a deft touch of just the briefest phrase; and in other passages, skillfully organized, he demonstrates his ability to handle rolling periods of a thunderous sonority. He can, and does, do just about anything with words and ideas except lull us into an indifferent tranquility. This amazingly versatile style poses tremendous problems for the translator who seeks to render in English the subtleties and nuances within the succinct suggestions and the lengthy developments that he presents in a uniquely personal accent but with an undeniably Gallic verve.

No one knows exactly how Pascal would have used these fragments had he completed his work on the truths of Christianity. The general outline of his proposed apology is, however, clear enough. Pascal is addressing himself to the intelligent, worldly nonbeliever. He has moved in circles of elegant society where atheistic ideas were freely expressed in drawing-room conversations. He has observed that in those circles the believer tends to assume a pose of indifference in matters of religion in order to conform to the moral and intellectual tone of the social group. To appreciate Pascal's intent, we must visualize the person he is addressing as a gentleman of the upper middle class or of the aristocracy; he has a superior education and is well read both in modern literatures and in the Latin classics; he frequents salons where he has developed skill in witty conversation and clever but superficial debate; he goes to the theater to see the tragedies of Corneille or Rotrou and the comedies of Scarron (Molière is about to return to Paris to write and perform his great comedies, and Racine has not yet revealed himself as a tragic poet); he has doubtless had military experience, and may very well have been involved in the rather silly revolts known as the *Fronde*; he is passionately fond of gambling and spends long hours at the gaming tables; he professes either atheism or a total indifference to religion.

Pascal wishes to seize his opponent, to shake him out of his smug complacency. And so he will startle him by offering to his imagination the staggering images of the realms of the infinitely great and the infinitely small. Having thus gained his attention, Pascal will seek to show him how meaningless life is if he remains in ignorance of God. No existentialist of the twentieth century has depicted in more vivid terms than Pascal the absurdity of man's lot. the emptiness and the anguish of his life so long as he is considered merely as an animal being in a material universe. His senses deceive him, his vaunted reason deludes him, his justice is merely a justification of force, he can know nothing but his nothingness. Man, so conceived, is a bewildering paradox, an incomprehensible monster.

Pascal hopes, by rapier thrusts that deflate man's pride and bludgeoning blows that destroy his identity, to make him willing to consider the means of escaping this absurdity. Life can become meaningful, he seeks to assure his reader, if only he will recognize the reality of the original sin that contaminates his nature and of grace, made accessible through Jesus Christ, which can restore him to that state from which he is fallen. But Pascal knows reason cannot prove these truths. Instead of positive proof, he offers to his gambling adversary a bet—and the central theme of the wager is introduced into the work. Pascal has no illusions about the intellectual value of the wager in arguing for an acceptance of belief, but he is not now addressing himself to the intelligence of his opponent. He asks him as a gambling man to consider what he may stand to lose or win in betting that God does exist; and then Pascal the mathematician, the expert in laws of probability, tells him that the odds are such that he is an utter fool not to gamble on His existence and to seek the Christian answer to the problems of life.

By bullying and cajoling, Pascal has now led his reader

to seek to attain faith through engaging in the practices of believers. What can he hope thus to attain? Pascal concludes his defense of the Christian religion by presenting Jesus Christ as the agent of our salvation and by suggesting the joys of the Christian life.

We are far indeed from the logically systematic arguments of the Scholastics or even of the *Discourse on Method*. But Pascal knows there are important areas of human experience in which reason cannot enter, and religion is one of these. Faith, he tells us, is a matter of the heart, not of the reason. His understanding of the complexity of life prevents his accepting and following anything so simple and rectilinear as conventional logic. We need not share his faith to recognize what a depth of understanding of the human mind and heart is in Pascal and to be stirred by his evocation of man's lot and by his mystic sense of the divine.

Pascal makes no effort to hide the borrowings that are frequent in the *Thoughts*. Originality, he tells us, consists in the manner in which ideas are combined rather than in the expression of ideas no one has ever conceived before. When he borrows from an author, he is not reducing the personal element in his work; he borrows precisely because he has recognized his own thought in what he reads. He is thoroughly steeped in the Bible and quotes it constantly. The *City of God* and other writings of St. Augustine are familiar to him. Like all educated men of his day, he can quote Vergil and Horace without referring to their books; and he is well acquainted with Lucretius and Epictetus. Next to the Bible, the one single book that has most deeply influenced him is Montaigne's *Essays*. He cites Montaigne directly or indirectly at every turn. Many developments in the *Thoughts* with regard to the inadequacy of man's reason, the unreliability of the senses, and the relativity of justice and truth are taken from "The Apology of Raymond Sebond," the longest of the essays. It is interesting to note that the one single author to whom he owes the most is also the one he most frequently attacks. Like every cultured Frenchman since the sixteenth century, he has read the *Essays* and meditated upon them; but to Pascal Montaigne's humanism seems impious. He criticizes Montaigne for the physical frankness of certain passages in his work, but this is merely in passing; what shocks him in Montaigne is a relative indifference to spiritual values and an apparent unconcern about eternity. Montaigne defends the Catholic faith, but on grounds that appear monstrous to Pascal: we should retain the faith of our fathers because we can never know the truth anyway, and the introduction of new beliefs and new practices causes dissension and leads (as Montaigne in sixteenth century France knew well from experience) to bloody civil wars. And so the author who most deeply influenced the thinking of Pascal is at the same time the author whom he most frequently and most roundly attacks.

In this selection of Pascal's *Thoughts*, an effort has been made to present them in some sort of logical sequence in order to suggest the development of a number of the major themes which would have figured in the author's proposed defense of the Christian faith. Pascal had not edited them; no one can claim to know just how he would have combined these elements of his projected work. Much of the strictly theological material is here omitted, as are most of the passages of Biblical commentary. It is proper to acknowledge the editor's debt to Jacques Chevalier whose excellent edition of the complete works of Pascal has greatly influenced the grouping followed in the presentation of these selections.

The translation is new. It follows the French text closely, taking few liberties except on occasion to break up some of the longest sentences in Pascal's text. No attempt has been made to conceal the weaknesses of style and organization which are to be expected in notes of such a random nature, hastily put down on paper as the author found the time or the inspiration. Some passages break off in the middle of a phrase; these are translated in the form in which Pascal in his haste left them.

It is hoped that some of the apparent contradictions encountered in traditional presentations of the *Thoughts* may disappear in the grouping of elements here employed. The occasional identification of passages in which not Pascal, but his opponent, is speaking may serve the same end. And above all it is hoped that, even viewed through the veil of translation, something of the illuminating penetration of Pascal's vision and something of the amazing spontaneity and startling vividness of Pascal's style may be perceptible.

The number in parentheses following each item is the number it bears in the Brunschvicg edition, long the classic edition of the *Thoughts*. Each Biblical quotation is followed by a chapter and verse reference given in brackets.

PRINCIPAL DATES
IN THE LIFE
OF BLAISE PASCAL

❧

1620   Birth of Gilberte Pascal, elder sister and future biographer of Blaise.

1623   June 19, birth of Blaise Pascal at Clermont where his father holds a judicial post.

1624   Prolonged illness of the infant Blaise, attributed to a "spell" cast by a witch.

1625   Birth of Jacqueline Pascal, sister of Blaise.

1626   Death of Antoinette Pascal, mother of Blaise.

1631   Étienne Pascal moves with his three children to Paris. A governess looks after the household, but the father personally directs the education of his children, to a great degree in accordance with the pedagogical principles of Montaigne. Precocious genius of Blaise, especially in mathematics.

1638   Étienne Pascal, in danger of imprisonment because of his opposition to a fiscal measure of Richelieu, retires to Auvergne, leaving his children in Paris.

1639   Jacqueline Pascal, after appearing in a play presented before Richelieu, obtains a pardon for her father, who is appointed royal collector of taxes in Rouen. Family moves to that city, capital of Normandy.

1640   First published work of Blaise Pascal, on conics.

1642   Blaise Pascal begins work on his calculating machine, designed to assist his father in his computation of taxes. The experimentation continues over the next decade, culminating in an efficient calculator. Pascal, not one to hide his light under a bushel, skillfully advertises and promotes his invention.

1646   Conversion to a severe Christianity of the Pascal household through the influence of two charitable gentlemen who care for Étienne Pascal after he has dislocated his hip. Late in the year, Blaise with his father repeats in Rouen the experiments on atmospheric pressure already conducted in Italy by Torricelli.

1647   Blaise Pascal, recuperating from a serious illness at the home of his sister in Paris, is visited twice by Descartes. Their opposing views on the vacuum and their conflicting temperaments soon lead to a breach that will never heal. Pascal, in collaboration with his brother-in-law, continues experiments on atmospheric pressure, disproving the classic assumption that "nature abhors a vacuum."

1648   Blaise Pascal writes a treatise on conic sections. Further publication on the problems of atmospheric pressure (the equilibrium of liquids).

1649   Pascal family returns to Clermont. Blaise works to refine his calculating machine.

1651   Back in Paris, Pascal is engaged in controversy concerning his work on atmospheric pressure and the vacuum.

1652   Jacqueline Pascal enters the Jansenist convent of Port-Royal. Beginning of a brief "worldly" period in the life of Blaise, in association with the Duke de Roannez, the Chevalier de Méré, and Damien Mitton.

1653   Writings on physics and mathematics.

1654   Night of November 23. Two hours of ecstatic illumination leading to Pascal's definitive conversion. From that time on, he is to keep a transcript of this mystic experience sewn inside the lining of his doublet.

1655   Pascal spends a retreat at Port-Royal.

1656   Arnauld, the spiritual head of Port-Royal, condemned by the faculty of theology. Pascal is drawn into the controversy. He defends the Jansenists and attacks the theological and moral laxity of the Jesuits in a brilliant series of eighteen "Provincial Letters," the last of which appears in June, 1657. March 24, the niece of Pascal cured miraculously of a fistula of a tear duct by the touch of a holy relic. Profound effect on Pascal. About this time, Pascal begins to work on his proposed apology (defense) of the Christian religion which will occupy much of his time for the next two years. The fragments left at his death form the *Pensées* (*Thoughts*) of Pascal.

1658   At Port-Royal, Pascal outlines to a group of friends his proposed apology.

1659   Grave illness, from which he will never recover. Intense suffering permitting only brief periods of work.

1661   The excellent school of Port-Royal closed as a consequence of the official condemnation of Jansenist doctrines. All members of the community ordered to abjure the teachings declared heretical. Jacqueline Pascal dies.

1662   August 17, Pascal dies. A postmortem examination reveals a serious gangrene of the intestine and also gangrenous areas in the brain.

1664-68   Great persecution of Jansenism.

1670   First edition of Pascal's *Thoughts*.

1709   Total destruction of Port-Royal.

Part I

THE STATE OF MAN
IN IGNORANCE OF GOD

SECTION A—GENERAL PLAN

1. The last thing one finds in preparing a work is to know what one should put first. (19)

2. Let it not be said that I have said nothing new; the arrangement of the materials is new. When two persons play tennis, it is the same ball that both play with, but one of them places it better.

I should just as soon be told that I have used old words. As if the same thoughts did not form a new expository development when arranged differently, just as the same words form other thoughts when arranged differently. (22)

3. Certain authors, talking about their works, say, "My book, my commentary, my history, etc." This smacks of the bourgeois who has a town house, and always in his mouth the words "My place." They would do better to say, "Our book, our commentary, our history, etc.," because normally there is more in it which belongs to other people than to them. (43)

4. *Order*—Men feel disdain for religion; they hold it in hatred, and fear that it may be true. To correct that, one must begin by showing that religion is not contrary to

1

reason, that it is to be revered. One must arouse respect for it, then present it in such a fashion as to make it loved, as to make good people wish it were true. Finally, one must show that it is true.

To be revered, because it has known well the nature of man; to be loved, because it promises the true good. (187)

5. Begin by pitying nonbelievers; they are sufficiently unfortunate because of their condition. You ought not to insult them, unless insulting might be useful to them; but insulting does them harm. (189)

6. Pity atheists who seek, for are they not sufficiently unfortunate? Rail against those who take pride in their atheism. (190)

7. The damned will be astounded to see that they will be condemned by their own reason, through which they sought to condemn the Christian faith. (563)

8. God's way, which arranges all things with gentleness, is to have religion enter the mind through reasonings, and the heart through grace. But to seek to put it into the mind and heart through force and threats, that is not to have religion enter there, but terror, terror rather than religion. (185)

9. In every dialogue and discourse, one must be able to say to those who take offense at it, "What are you complaining about?" (188)

10. It is dangerous to make man see too clearly how like he is to the beasts, without revealing to him likewise his greatness. It is dangerous also to show him too clearly his greatness without his baseness. It is even more dangerous to leave him in ignorance of both. But it is most advantageous to present both to him.

Man must not believe that he is like the beasts, nor like the angels; he must not be ignorant of either, but he must know both. (418)

11. If he is boastful, I deflate him; if he belittles himself, I praise him; and I contradict him always, until he recognizes that he is an incomprehensible monster. (420)

12. *Contradictions: after showing the baseness and the greatness of man*—Let man now consider his true worth. Let him love himself, for there is in him a nature capable of good; but let him not love for that reason the baseness that is in him. Let him despise himself, because the capacity is empty; but let him not despise for that reason that natural capacity. Let him hate himself, let him love himself—he has within him the power to know the truth and to be happy; but he has no truth that is constant or satisfying.

I should like, then, to bring man to desire to find the truth, to be ready, and freed from passions, to follow it wherever he may find it, knowing to what degree his knowledge has been obscured by passions. I should like him to hate within himself the lust which sways him by itself so that it may not blind him in making his choice and may not stop him when he has made it. (423)

SECTION B—THE TWO INFINITES

13. *Man's disproportion*—That is where natural knowledge leads us. If such knowledge is not real, there is no truth in man; and if it is, he finds in it a great cause of humiliation, forced to demean himself in either case. And since his very being requires him to accept natural knowledge, before undertaking more extensive research into nature, I wish that he might for once consider it seriously and at leisure, that he might examine himself also, and knowing his true proportion. . . .

Let man contemplate, then, the whole of nature in its

lofty and full majesty; let him turn aside his gaze from the mean objects which surround him. Let him look upon that dazzling light, set like an eternal lamp to illumine the universe; let the earth appear to him as a mere point in comparison with the vast circuit which that orb follows; and let him realize with amazement that that vast orbit itself is only a very minute point in relation to the distances traversed by the stars which roll through the firmament. But if our sight can go no farther, let the imagination pass beyond; it will weary of conceiving before nature will be exhausted in furnishing food to the imagination. The whole visible universe is only an imperceptible dot in the ample expanse of nature. No idea of ours can come near it. It does us no good to extend our conceptions beyond imaginable spaces; we give birth to mere atoms in comparison with the reality of things. Nature is an infinite sphere whose center is everywhere, whose circumference is nowhere. Ultimately, it is the greatest perceptible feature of God's almightiness that our imagination should be lost in that thought.

Let man, coming back to himself, consider what he is in comparison with what is; let him consider himself as lost in this out-of-the-way corner of nature; and from this little cell in which he finds himself lodged (I mean our universe) let him learn to appreciate at their true worth the world, the kingdoms, the cities, and himself. What is man within the infinite?

But to present to him another marvel just as astonishing, let him seek in what he knows the most minute things. Let a mite offer him, in the minuteness of its body, parts incomparably smaller, limbs with joints, veins in its limbs, blood in its veins, humors in that blood, drops in those humors, vapors in those drops; then dividing these last things, let him exhaust his powers of imagination, and let the last object which he can reach be now the subject of our discussion; he will think, perhaps, that there cannot possibly be within nature anything more minute. I want to show him within that object a new abyss. I want to paint for him not only the visible universe, but the immensity of nature which one can imagine within the limits of that fragment of an atom. Let him see within it an infinity of universes, each of which has its firmament, its planets, its earth, in the same proportion as the visible world; let him see in that earth animals, and ultimately mites in which he will find again what the first ones offered; and finding again in the others the same thing, endlessly and tirelessly, let him lose himself in these marvels, as astonishing in their minuteness as the others in their magnitude. For who will not marvel that our body, which a moment ago was not perceptible in the universe, imperceptible itself within the bosom of the whole, should be now a colossus, a world, or rather an all, in relation to the nothingness which one can reach?

Whoever will consider himself thus will grow frightened of himself, and, considering himself suspended in the mass which nature has given him between these two abysses of the infinitely great and the infinitely small, he will tremble at the sight of these marvels; and I believe that, his curiosity changing into marvelment, he will be more disposed to contemplate them in silence than to seek them out with presumption.

For after all, what is man in nature? A mere nothing in comparison with the infinite, an all in comparison with the infinitely small, a midpoint between nothing and everything. Infinitely far from grasping the extremes, the end of things and their beginning are for him invincibly hidden in an impenetrable secret; and he is equally incapable of seeing the nothingness out of which he is drawn, and the infinite in which he is swallowed up.

What will he do, then, except form a faint idea of the mean of things, in an eternal despair of knowing either their principle or their end? All things proceed out of nothingness and are borne toward infinity. Who will follow this astonishing progression? The author of these marvels understands them; no other can do so.

Because they had failed to contemplate these infinites,

men have rashly set about an examination of nature as though it could be brought within their grasp. It is a strange thing that they have sought to understand the principles of things, and from that beginning to succeed in understanding the whole. Their presumption is as infinite as their objective. For it is beyond doubt that one cannot undertake such a plan without infinite presumption, or without a capacity infinite as nature itself.

The informed person recognizes that nature has left its imprint and that of its author on all things; and almost all, therefore, share nature's twofold infinity. It is thus that we see all sciences to be infinite in the range of their possible research, for who doubts that geometry, for example, has an infinite infinity of problems to develop? They are likewise infinite in the multitude and minuteness of their premises, for who does not see that those which are offered as fundamental do not stand by themselves and are supported by others which, supported by still others in turn, never permit reaching any true first principle? But we treat the ultimate principles perceptible to our reason as we treat the smallest visible material things, considering as indivisible that point beyond which our senses perceive nothing more, even though it be by its nature infinitely divisible.

Of these two infinites of science, the infinitely great is much more readily felt, and that is why few men have claimed to know everything. "I am going to speak of everything," said Democritus.

But the infinitely small is much less visible. Philosophers have much more frequently claimed to reach it, and that is where all have stumbled. That is what has given rise to such frequent titles as *Principles of Things, Principles of Philosophy,* and so on, as pretentious in fact, though less so in appearance, as that title of self-evident absurdity, *Of All Things Knowable*.

Naturally we think ourselves more capable of reaching the center of things than of embracing their circumference. The visible expanse of the universe is visibly beyond our grasp. But since we surpass in size small things, we believe ourselves more capable of mastering them; and yet it requires no less capacity to reach the infinitely small than to reach the infinitely great. In either case it takes an infinite intelligence, and it seems to me that anyone who could have understood the ultimate principles of things could just as well succeed in knowing the infinite. One depends on the other, and one leads to the other. These extremities are contiguous and join one another by virtue of being so far apart, and meet in God and in God alone.

Let us then recognize our scope. We are something, and we are not everything. What being we have prevents our having knowledge of first principles, which are born out of nothingness; and its pettiness hides from us a view of the infinite.

Our intelligence occupies in the order of intelligible things the same rank as our body in the vastness of nature.

Limited in all respects, this state which occupies a mid-position between two extremes prevails in all our faculties. Our senses perceive nothing extreme. Too much sound deafens us, too much light dazzles us, too great a distance and too close proximity prevent us from seeing, too much length and too much brevity keep us from following an argument, too much truth baffles us (I know some who cannot understand that if you subtract four from zero, zero remains). First principles are too obvious for us. Too much pleasure wearies us, too many harmonies are unpleasant in music, and too many favors annoy us. We wish to be in a position to overpay the debt: "Favors bestowed are welcome so long as we believe we can repay them; if they much exceed that limit, gratitude gives place to resentment." [1] We feel neither extreme heat nor extreme cold. Good qualities in excess are inimical to us and cannot be perceived; we no longer feel them, we suffer them. Too much youth and too much age hinder the mind, as do too much or too little instruction. Finally, extremes are for us

[1] Tacitus, *Annals* IV, 18; Montaigne III, 8.

as if they did not exist at all, and we do not exist so far as they are concerned. They elude us, or we elude them.

That is our true state. That is what makes us incapable of knowing with certainty, or of remaining absolutely ignorant. We float over a vast middle area, always uncertain and drifting, driven from one end toward the other. Whenever we hope to moor ourselves and tie up to some point, it stirs and leaves us; and if we follow it, it escapes our grasp, eludes us, and flees in eternal flight. Nothing stops for us. That is our natural state, though utterly contrary to our inclination. We ardently desire to find a firm foundation, and at last a constant base upon which to erect a tower rising to infinity. But all our foundation cracks, and the earth opens to its very depths.

Let us then seek no security and no stability. Our reason is always deceived by the inconstancy of appearances. Nothing can fix the finite between the two infinites which enclose it and which escape its grasp.

That being clearly understood, I believe we shall remain at rest, each in the state in which nature placed him. This middle ground which is allotted to us being always distant from the extremes, what does it matter if another have a little more understanding of things? If he has, he simply grasps them a bit higher. Is he not still infinitely distant from the end, and is not the duration of our life still infinitesimal within eternity, even if ten years be added to it?

In comparison with these infinites, all finites are equal, and I see no reason to base my imagination upon one finite rather than another. Any comparison that we make of ourselves with the finite is painful.

If man studied himself first, he would see how incapable he is of going beyond himself. How could a part know the whole? But he will aspire perhaps to know at least those parts which are of a comparable proportion? But the parts of the world are all so interrelated and bound up one with another that I think it impossible to know one without the other and without the whole.

Man, for example, is linked with everything he knows. He needs space to contain him, time to give him duration, movement in order to live, elements to compose his body, warmth and food to nourish it, air to breathe. He sees light, he feels bodies. In short, everything has some relationship with him. In order to know man, we must then know how it comes that he needs air in order to live; and, to know air, we must know how it has acquired this relationship to the life of man, etc. Fire cannot exist without air; thus, to know one, we must know the other.

Thus all things being caused and causing, aided and aiding, mediate or immediate, and all supporting one another by a natural and imperceptible bond which links the most distant and the most different, I maintain that it is impossible to know the parts without knowing the whole, just as it is impossible to know the whole without knowing the parts one by one.

The eternity of things in itself or in God must likewise astonish our brief duration. The fixed and constant immobility of nature in comparison with the continual change which takes place in us must produce the same effect.

And what completes our incapacity to know things is that they are simple, whereas we are compounded of two natures, opposite and differing in kind: body and soul. For it is impossible that the reasoning part in us should be anything but spiritual; and even though one might claim that we are simply corporeal, that would exclude us much more from the knowledge of things, there being nothing so inconceivable as to declare that matter knows itself. It is impossible for us to know how it might know itself.

And thus if we are merely material we can know nothing at all, and if we are compounded of spirit and matter we cannot know simple things perfectly, whether they be spiritual or corporeal.

Thence it comes that almost all philosophers confuse things in their thinking, and talk in spiritual terms about material things, and in material terms about spiritual things. For they assert boldly that bodies tend to fall, that they seek their center, that they flee their destruction, that they fear the void, that they have inclinations, sympathies, antipathies, which are all things that belong only to spirits. And speaking of spirits, they consider them as occupying a certain place, and attribute to them movement from one spot to another, which are things pertaining only to bodies.

Instead of receiving the ideas of these things without adulteration, we color with our own qualities and stamp with the features of our own composite nature all the simple things which we contemplate.

Who would not believe, seeing us compound in all things spirit and body, that that mixture would be quite comprehensible to us? And yet that is precisely what we understand the least. Man is for himself the most prodigious object of nature, for he cannot conceive what body is, and even less what spirit is, and least of all how a body can be united to a spirit. This is man's crowning difficulty, and yet it is his own being: "The way in which spirit is joined to body cannot be understood by man, and yet this is what man is."[2] (72)

14. When I consider the short span of my life, absorbed in the eternity which precedes and the eternity which follows it, the little space that I fill, and even the space I see, swallowed up in the infinite immensity of the spaces which I know not and which know not me, I am frightened and astonished to see myself here rather than there, for there is no reason why here rather than there, why now rather than then. Who put me here? By whose order and act were this time and place destined for me? "As the remembrance of a guest of one day that passeth by." [The Wisdom of Solomon V, 15] (205)

15. How many kingdoms ignore our existence! (207)

16. The eternal silence of these infinite spaces frightens me. (206)

[2] Augustine, *City of God* XXI, 10.

SECTION C—THE SELF

17. What is the self?

A man stands by his window to watch the passersby. If I pass that way, can I say that he took up that position in order to see me? No, for he is not thinking of me in particular. But he who loves a woman because of her beauty, does he love her? No, for smallpox, which will destroy beauty without destroying the person, will result in his no longer loving her.

And if someone loves me for my judgment, for my memory, am I loved for my self? No, for I can lose those qualities without losing my self. Where then is that self, if it is neither in the body nor in the soul? And how can one love the body or the soul except for those qualities which are not what constitute the self, since they are perishable? For would one love the substance of a person's soul in an abstract fashion and without regard to the qualities that reside in it? That is not possible, and would be unjust. We never love anyone, then, but only qualities.

Let us no longer ridicule those who have themselves honored for their positions and offices, for we love no one except for borrowed qualities. (323)

18. You must know yourself; even though that knowledge serves in no wise to find the truth, at least it serves to help you regulate your life, and there is nothing more appropriate. (66)

19. It is not in Montaigne, but in myself, that I find everything I see in his book. (64)

20. What is good in Montaigne can be acquired only with difficulty. What is bad in him (I mean apart from moral attitudes) could have been corrected in a moment if he had been warned that he told too many stories, and that he talked too much about himself. (65)

21. How disordered our judgment is, since there is no one who does not place himself above all the rest of the world, and who does not prefer his own good, and the preservation of his happiness and of his life, to that of all the rest of the world. (456)

22. Each man judges everything in terms of his own being, for with his death everything perishes so far as he is concerned. Thence it comes that each thinks he is everything for everyone. We must not judge nature in relation to ourselves, but as it is in itself. (417)

23. We do not find sufficient the life that we have in us and in our own being; we wish to live in the minds of other people with an imaginary life, and we strive for that reason to put on a front. We work incessantly to embellish and preserve our imaginary being, and we neglect the real one. And if we have either tranquility, or generosity, or fidelity, we hasten to make it known, in order to attach those virtues to our other being; and we would detach them rather from ourselves so that we might join them to that other; we would not hesitate to act as cowards if by so doing we might acquire the reputation of being valiant. What a great mark of the nothingness of our own being that we are not satisfied with the real being without the imaginary one, and frequently exchange one for the other! For he who would not die to keep his honor would be infamous. (147)

24. *Pride*—Curiosity is only vanity. Usually we want to acquire knowledge only so that we may talk about it; otherwise we would not travel over the sea if we could never say anything about it, and for the sole pleasure of seeing, without hope of ever communicating to others what we had seen. (152)

25. *On the desire to be esteemed by those about us*— Pride holds us with such a natural possession in the midst

of our miseries, errors, etc. We even give up our life with joy, if only people talk about it.

Vanity: gambling, hunting, visits, the theater, false perpetuation of one's name. (153)

26. We are so presumptuous that we should wish to be known to the whole world, and even to people who will come when we are no more; and we are so vain that the esteem of five or six persons around us delights and satisfies us. (148)

27. We do not worry about being esteemed in towns through which we merely pass. But, when we are to stay a short time in a place, we do worry about it. How much time is needed? A time proportionate to our vain and puny span of life. (149)

28. Vanity is so deeply anchored in the heart of man that a common soldier, a camp follower, a porter are boastful and wish to have their admirers; and even philosophers want admirers; and those who write against them want to have the glory of having written well; and those who read them want to have the glory of having read them; and I, who am writing this, have perhaps that same desire; and perhaps those who will read me. . . . (150)

29. *Pursuits*—The appeal of glory is so great that no matter what gives rise to it, even if it be death, we still love it. (158)

30. Time heals wounds and quarrels because people change, they are no longer the same persons. Neither the offender nor the offended is any longer himself. It is like a nation which one has offended and which one would see again after two generations. They are still Frenchmen, but not the same ones. (122)

31. He no longer loves this person whom he loved ten years ago. I should think not; she is no longer the same,

nor is he. He was young, and she too; she is quite
different. He would perhaps love her now as she was then.
(123)

32. Not only do we look at things from different angles,
but with other eyes; we do not seek to find them identical.
(124)

33. The nature of self-love and of this human ego is to
love only oneself and to consider only oneself. But what
will man do? He cannot prevent this object he loves being
full of faults and miseries: he aspires to greatness, and he
sees himself small; he wants to be happy, and he sees
himself wretched; he wants to be perfect, and he sees
himself full of imperfections; he wants to be the object of
the love and esteem of men, and he sees that his faults
merit only their aversion and their disdain. This embarrass-
ment in which he finds himself produces in him the most
unjust and most criminal passion that it is possible to imagine. For he conceives a mortal hatred against that truth
which reproves him, and which convinces him of his
faults. He would like to annihilate it; and, unable to destroy it in itself, he destroys it, in so far as he is able,
within his own knowledge and that of others—that is to
say that he puts forth every effort to conceal his faults
from others and from himself, and that he cannot abide
that anyone should reveal them to himself or even see
them.

It is doubtless an evil to be full of faults; but it is still a
greater one to be full of them and to refuse to recognize
them, since that means adding to them the additional fault
of willful illusion. We do not wish others to deceive us; we
think it unjust that they should seek from us a greater
esteem than they merit; it is not, then, any more just for us
to deceive them and to seek from them a greater esteem
than we deserve.

Thus, when they discover only imperfections and vices
which we do indeed have, it is obvious that they are doing

us no wrong, since they are not the ones responsible; it is even obvious that they are doing us good, for they are helping us to free ourselves from an evil, which is our ignorance of these imperfections. We ought not to be annoyed that they know them, and that they hold us in disdain; is it not just both that they should know us for what we are, and that they should hold us in disdain if indeed we merit it?

Those are the ideas which would rise in a heart that would be full of equity and justice. What must we say of our own heart, finding in it a quite contrary disposition? For is it not true that we hate the truth and those who reveal it to us, and that we like them to be deceived to our advantage, and that we wish to be considered by them other than what we really are?

Here is a proof of it which horrifies me. The Catholic religion does not obligate us to reveal our sins indifferently to everyone. It permits us to hide ourselves from all other men; but it makes a single exception to whom it commands us to reveal the hidden recesses of our heart, and to show ourselves as we are. There is only this one man in all the world that it orders us not to deceive; and it obliges him to inviolable secrecy, with the result that this knowledge is in him as if it were not there. Can one imagine anything more charitable and more gentle? And yet such is the corruption of man that he finds harshness even in this law, and it is one of the principal reasons which led a large part of Europe to revolt against the Church.

How unjust and unreasonable is the heart of man if he objects to being obliged to do in the case of one man what it would be just, in a sense, to do in the case of all men! For is it just that we should deceive them?

There are different degrees in this aversion for truth, but it may be said that it is in all persons in some degree because it is inseparable from self-love. It is this false sensitivity which obliges those who are under the necessity of correcting others to choose so many detours and to proceed so gingerly in order to avoid offending them. They must play down our faults, pretend to excuse them, mix with their reproofs praise and displays of affection and esteem. In spite of that, this medicine is still a bitter dose for our self-love which takes the least of it possible, and always with disgust, and often even with a secret annoyance against those who present it.

As a consequence, it happens that if someone has some wish to win our affection, he will turn away from rendering us a service which he knows will be displeasing to us. He will treat us as we wish to be treated. We hate the truth, and so he hides it from us; we wish to be flattered, and so he flatters us; we like to be deceived, and so he deceives us.

That is why each degree of good fortune which raises us in the world moves us farther away from the truth, for people fear offending others in proportion as their affection is more useful and their enmity more dangerous. A prince will be the laughingstock of all Europe, and he alone will know nothing about it. I am not surprised at that; to tell the truth is useful to the one to whom one tells it, but disadvantageous to those who tell it, because they arouse hatred against themselves. Now those who live with princes place their own interests above those of the prince they serve, and thus they are careful not to procure him an advantage if it means harming themselves.

This misfortune is doubtless greater and more usual in the case of people of great wealth; but others are not exempt, because there is always something to be gained by making oneself loved by men. Thus human life is only a perpetual illusion; people are constantly engaged in mutual deception and flattery. Nobody talks about us in our presence as he does in our absence. The union which exists among men is founded only upon this mutual deceiving. Few friendships would remain if each knew what his friend says of him when he is not there, although his friend talks of him then sincerely and dispassionately.

Man then is nothing but disguise, falsehood, and hypocrisy both in himself and with regard to others. He does not wish to have the truth told to him; he avoids saying it to others; and all these inclinations, so contrary to justice and reason, have a natural root in his heart. (100)

34. To pity the unfortunate is not against selfish interest. On the contrary, we are delighted to have the opportunity to offer this evidence of friendship and to draw on ourselves the reputation of tenderness, without giving anything. (452)

35. All men naturally hate one another. They have used selfish interest as best they could to make it serve the public good, but this is only a pretense and a false image of charity, for at bottom there is only hatred. (451)

36. "The ego is hateful. You, Mitton,[3] conceal your ego; you do not remove it for all that; you are therefore always hateful."—"Not at all, for by acting as we do, in an obliging fashion toward everyone, people have no reason to hate us."—"That is true, if one hated in the ego only the harm it causes for us. But if I hate it because it is unjust, because it makes itself the center of everything, I shall always hate it."

In a word, the ego has two qualities. It is unjust in itself in that it makes itself the center of everything. It is offensive to others, in that it seeks to enslave them; for each ego is the enemy of, and would like to be the tyrant over, all others. You remove its offensiveness, but not its injustice. Thus you do not make it admirable to those who hate its injustice; you make it admirable only to the unjust who no longer find in it their enemy, and in this way you remain unjust and cannot please the just. (455)

SECTION D—HUMAN REASON AND JUDGMENT

37. Those who judge of a work without any rules to follow are, in comparison with the others, like those who

[3] Mitton—close personal friend of Pascal and companion of his worldly period.

have a watch in comparison with the others. One says, "It has been two hours," while another says, "It has been only three-quarters of an hour." I consult my watch, and I say to the first, "You are bored," and to the second, "Time is flying swiftly for you," for it has been an hour and a half. I do not care about those who tell me that time drags by for me, and that I am judging it by caprice; they do not know that I am judging it by my watch. (5)

38. *Distinction between the mathematical and the discerning mind*—In the first, the principles are palpable, but far removed from common usage, so that one has difficulty turning one's head in their direction for lack of practice. But as soon as one does consider them, one sees the principles fully; one would have to have a mind incapable of functioning properly to reason ill upon principles so clear that it is almost impossible for them to escape us.

In the discerning mind, the principles are in common usage and everyone has them before him. You need not turn your head, nor make any effort of application; it is enough to have clear vision, but it must be really clear for the principles are so subtle and so numerous that you are almost certain to overlook some. Now the omission of a principle leads to error; thus you must be very clearsighted to see all the principles, and then you must have a very precise mind to avoid drawing false conclusions from known principles.

All geometricians would then be discerning thinkers if they were clearsighted, for they do not draw false conclusions from the principles which they know; and the discerning thinkers would be capable of mathematical reasoning if they could bring their attention to bear on the unaccustomed principles of geometry.

The reason why certain discerning minds are not mathematicians is that they cannot at all bring themselves to consider the principles of geometry; but what keeps mathematicians from attaining discernment is that they do not see what is before them, and being accustomed only to the precise and obvious principles of geometry, and to reasoning only after seeing clearly and handling their principles, they are lost in matters of discernment where principles cannot be handled in the same way. You scarcely see these principles, you feel them rather than perceive them. You have infinite difficulty in getting people who do not intuitively feel them to recognize them. They are so delicate and so numerous that you must have a very delicate and clear sensitivity to feel them; and you must judge aright and with precision according to that feeling, usually without being able to prove them in an orderly fashion as in geometry because you do not possess these principles in the same way and it would be an infinitely difficult undertaking. You must without hesitation see the thing in a single glance, and not by progressive reasoning, at least up to a certain degree. And thus it is rare that geometricians are discerning, and that intuitive minds are mathematical, because geometricians insist on treating these matters of discernment in a geometric way and make themselves ridiculous, seeking to begin by definitions and then by principles, which is not the way of acting in this kind of reasoning. It is not that the mind does not reason, but it does so tacitly, naturally, and without art; for it is beyond all men to express this mode of thought, and it is given only to a few to possess this intuition.

And discerning minds, on the contrary, being thus accustomed to judging at a single glance, are so bewildered when they encounter propositions in which they understand nothing, and which can be approached only with recourse to those sterile definitions and principles which they are inexperienced in examining in detail, that they grow discouraged and give up in disgust.

But inept minds are never either discerning or mathematical.

Geometricians who are nothing but geometricians have then an accurate mind, but only if you explain everything to them by definitions and principles; otherwise they are inept and unbearable, for they are exact only when dealing with perfectly clear principles.

And discerning minds which are nothing but discerning cannot have the patience to probe to the first principles of matters of speculation and imagination which they have never seen in the world and which are quite beyond their experience. (1)

39. *Geometry, discernment*—True eloquence disdains eloquence, true morality disdains morality; that is to say that the morality of the judgment, which has no rules, disdains the morality of the reason.

For to the realm of judgment belongs feeling, as the sciences belong to the realm of reason. Intuition is of the domain of judgment as geometry is of the domain of reason.

To disdain philosophy is really to be a philosopher. (4)

40. Those who are accustomed to judge by feeling understand nothing in matters of reasoning, for they wish immediately to get to the heart of a problem in one glance and are not accustomed to seeking principles. And the others, on the contrary, who are accustomed to reasoning according to principles, understand nothing in matters of feeling, seeking to find principles and unable to see at a glance. (3)

41. Diversity is so great that all tones of voice, ways of walking, or coughing, or blowing the nose, or sneezing . . . We distinguish grapes from other fruits, and among grapes the muscat varieties, and then the Condrieu, the Desargues, and ultimately this vine. Is that all? Has this vine ever produced two identical clusters? And does a cluster have two identical grapes? Etc.

I have never twice judged the same thing in exactly the same way. I cannot judge my work as I am producing it; I must do as painters do, and I must step back from it, but not too far. How much then? You have to guess. (114)

42. If one is too young, one does not judge well; the same is true if one is too old. If one does not think enough about a problem, or if one thinks too much about it, one grows stubborn, and one persists in his error. If an author considers his work straightway after completing it, he is still quite prejudiced about it; if he waits too long, it seems foreign to him. Thus with paintings, seen from too far away and too close up. There is only one indivisible point that is the true position from which to view each one; the others are too near, too far, too high, or too low. Perspective assigns that place in the art of painting. But in matters of truth and morality, who will assign it? (381)

43. There is a universal and essential difference between the actions of the will and all others.

The will is one of the principal organs of belief, not that it forms belief, but because things are true or false depending on the aspect by which we view them. The will, which approves one aspect more than another, dissuades the mind from considering the qualities of those aspects which it does not like to see; and thus the mind, advancing in step with the will, stops to consider the aspect preferred by the will, and so it judges by what it sees there. (99)

44. The mind of this sovereign judge of the world is not so independent that it is not subject to being disturbed by the first hubbub that occurs about him. It does not take the sound of a cannon to disturb his thoughts; it takes only the sound of a weather vane or a pulley. Do not be surprised that he is reasoning so badly now; a fly is buzzing about his ears. That is enough to make him incapable of good counsel. If you wish him to find the truth, shoo away that creature which undoes his reason and disturbs that powerful intelligence which governs cities and kingdoms.

What an amusing god that is! O most ridiculous hero!
(366)

45. The power of flies: they win battles, prevent our mind from functioning, devour our body. (367)

46. *Imagination*—It is that controlling factor in man, that mistress of error and falsity, and all the more treacherous because it is not always so; it would be an infallible touchstone of truth if it were an infallible touchstone of falsehood. But, being most commonly false, it gives no mark of its quality, marking with the same stamp both the true and the false.

I am not talking about madness, I am talking about the wisest of men; and it is among them that imagination has the great privilege of persuading men. It does reason no good to protest; reason cannot determine the worth of things.

That superb power, the enemy of reason, which delights in controlling and dominating it in order to demonstrate what it can do in all things, has established in man a second nature. Imagination makes people happy or unhappy, healthy or ill, rich or poor; it inspires belief or doubt, and it contradicts reason; it conceals meanings, or makes them obvious; it has its fools and its sages; and nothing disturbs us more than to see that it fills its hosts with a satisfaction incomparably more full and complete than does reason. Those who are clever through imagination look upon themselves with much more satisfaction than prudent people can reasonably do. They look upon others imperiously; they argue boldly and confidently, while others argue with fear and distrust. This gaiety of countenance gives them often the advantage in the opinion of those who listen, so much favor do these imaginary sages find in the minds of judges similarly constituted. Imagination cannot make fools wise, but it makes them happy, to the envy of reason which can make its favorites only miserable; the one covering them with glory, the other with shame.

Who dispenses reputation? What gives respect and veneration to persons, to works, to laws, to the great, unless it be this faculty of imagination? How inadequate all the wealth of the earth appears without its consent!

Would you not say that this magistrate, whose venerable old age imposes respect upon a whole nation, is governed by a pure and sublime reason and that he judges things by their true nature without lingering over those vain circumstances which attack only the imagination of the weak? See him attend a church service to which he brings a most devout zeal, strengthening the solidity of his reason by the ardor of his charity. There he is, ready to listen to the sermon with an exemplary respect. Now let the preacher appear; if nature has given him a hoarse voice and a strange cast of countenance, if his barber has shaved him ill, if by chance he is spotted with dirt, whatever great truths he may set forth, I will wager that our senator will have lost his gravity.

The greatest philosopher in the world, on a plank broader than necessary, if he sees an abyss beneath him, although his reason persuades him of his safety, his imagination will prevail. Some could not even endure the thought without turning pale and breaking into a sweat.

I do not wish to report all the effects of imagination.

Who does not know people for whom the sight of cats or rats, the crushing of a coal, etc., is sufficient to unhinge their reason? The tone of voice influences the wisest persons, and alters the effect of a speech and a poem.

Affection or hatred make justice change sides. And how much more just a lawyer finds the cause he is pleading if he has been well paid in advance! How much better his bold gesture makes it appear to the judges, duped by this appearance. A strange reason that a breath of air can sway, and in any direction.

I should record almost all actions of men, for they are

scarcely stirred except by the stimulus of imagination. For reason has been obliged to yield, and the wisest reason takes for its principles the very ones that the imagination of men has boldly introduced everywhere.

He who would wish to follow only reason would be mad in the judgment of the majority of people. One must, because it has pleased these people, work all day long for goods recognized as imaginary; and when sleep has lifted from us the fatigue of our reason, we must straightway rise with a bound to chase after the elusive glory and undergo the impressions of this mistress of the world. That is one of the principles of error, but it is not the only one. Man has been well advised to ally these two powers, although in that peace imagination has very fully the advantage. When imagination and reason are at war, the former prevails much more completely; never does reason entirely triumph over imagination, whereas imagination often unseats entirely reason from its throne.

Our magistrates have well recognized this mystery. Their red robes, their ermine, in which they wrap themselves up like furry cats, the palaces where they sit in judgment, the fleur-de-lis, all those august trappings were indeed necessary; and if physicians did not wear cassocks and mules, and if jurists did not have square bonnets and robes four times fuller than necessary, they would never have duped society which cannot resist so authentic a display. If lawyers had real justice and if physicians had the true art of healing, they would have no need of square bonnets; the majesty of these sciences would be sufficiently venerable in itself. But possessing only imaginary sciences, they must adopt these vain accessories which strike the imagination with which they deal; and in this manner, indeed, they draw respect upon themselves. Only military persons are not disguised thus, because indeed their importance is of their very essence; they establish themselves by force, the others by appearance.

This is why our kings have not sought these disguises. They have not masked themselves with extraordinary clothes in order to appear as kings, but they have themselves accompanied by guards, by crossbowmen. These armed troops who have hands and strength only for them, and those legions which surround them, make the boldest tremble. They do not have merely the robes, they do indeed have force. One would have to have a singularly unprejudiced reason to look as one would on any other man upon the Turkish monarch surrounded, in his superb harem, by forty thousand janissaries.

We cannot even see a lawyer in his robe and with his bonnet on his head without an advantageous opinion of his competence.

Imagination controls everything; it makes beauty, justice, happiness (which is the world's highest good). I should eagerly like to see the Italian book which I know only by title, but that title in itself is worth many books: *On Opinion, Queen of the World.* I endorse it sight unseen, except for the evil, if evil there be, in it.

Those are more or less the effects of that deceitful faculty which seems to have been given us on purpose to lead us to a necessary error. We have many other sources of error.

Old impressions are not alone capable of deceiving us; the charms of novelty have the same power. Thence come all the disputes of men who reproach one another either with following their false impressions of childhood, or with running boldly after new ones. Who can hit the golden mean? Let him appear, and let him prove it. There is no principle, however natural it may be, even in childhood, that one does not accuse of being a false impression either as a consequence of instruction or of the error of the senses.

"Because," they say, "you have believed from childhood that a chest was empty when you saw nothing in it, you have believed the void possible. It is an illusion of your senses, fortified by custom, which science must correct." And the others say: "Because they have told you in school that there is no void, they have corrupted your common sense, which understood the void so clearly before that false instruction, which you must now correct by going back to your first nature." Who, then, has deceived? The senses, or instruction?

We have another source of error, illnesses. They spoil our judgment and affect our senses; and if great ones alter our judgment appreciably, I do not doubt that slight ones make their impression on it in their due proportion.

Our own interest is also a marvelous instrument for blinding our eyes pleasantly. It is not permitted the most equitable man in the world to be judge in his own cause; I know some who, to avoid falling into that self-love, have been totally unjust in matters affecting themselves. The sure way to lose an entirely just case was to have it recommended to them by their close relatives.

Justice and truth are two such subtle matters that our instruments are too blunt to touch them exactly. If they succeed at all, they cover up the point, and press all about, more on the false than on the true. (82)

47. Our imagination magnifies so much the present time, by dint of reflecting so continually upon it, and so diminishes eternity through our failure to reflect upon it, that we reduce eternity to nothingness, and out of the nothingness of the present we make an eternity; and all that has its roots so deep within us that our reason cannot protect us against it. (195 *bis*)

48. Imagination magnifies little objects to the point of filling our soul with them by fantastically exaggerating their importance; and, with a rash insolence, it reduces great things to its measure, as when we talk of God. (84)

49. The thing to which we attribute the most importance, such as hiding our little worth, is often almost nothing. It is a nothing that our imagination magnifies into a mountain. Another trick of imagination makes us discover it without difficulty. (85)

50. My fancy makes me hate a man with a croaking voice and one who breathes heavily while eating. Fancy has great weight. What profit shall we draw from that fact? Should we follow that inclination because it is natural? No, we should conclude rather to resist it. (86)

51. Children who are frightened at the face they have blackened, they are but children; but how can what is weak in childhood be very strong at a later age? One only changes one's fancy. Everything that is perfected progressively perishes progressively. Whatever has been weak can never be completely strong. It does no good to say, "He has grown, he is changed"; he is also the same. (88)

52. If we dreamed every night the same thing, it would affect us as much as the objects that we see every day. And if a craftsman were sure of dreaming every night, for a full twelve hours, that he was king, I think he would be almost as happy as a king who could dream that he was a craftsman.

Were we to dream every night that we were pursued by enemies, and agitated by these terrifying phantoms, and were we to spend every day occupied in numerous ways as when we travel, we should suffer almost as much as if our dreams were true; and we should dread falling asleep as we dread waking up when we fear encountering such misfortunes in reality. And indeed that would produce almost the same ills as the reality.

But because dreams are all different, and even the same one takes various forms, what we see in dreams affects us much less than what we see when awake because of the continuity, which is however not so continuous and even that it does not change also, but less suddenly, unless it be on rare occasions as when we are traveling. And then we say, "It seems to me I am dreaming," for life is a dream a little less swiftly moving. (386)

53. M. de Roannez[4] used to say, "Reasons come to me afterwards, but first the thing pleases me or shocks me without my knowing the reason, and yet it shocks me for that very reason that I discover only later." But I believe, not that it shocked for those reasons that one recognizes afterwards, but that one finds those reasons because the thing shocks him. (276)

54. *Spongia solis*[5]—When we see an effect always occur in the same way, we conclude from it a natural necessity, as that dawn will come tomorrow, etc. But often nature plays us false, and is not subject to its own rules. (91)

55. When the truth concerning a matter is not known, it is good that there should be a common error which the minds of men can accept, as, for example, the moon to which are attributed the changes of the seasons, the progress of maladies, etc. The principal malady of man is the disturbing curiosity concerning things he cannot know, and it is less bad for him to be in error than a prey to that useless curiosity. (18)

56. Memory is necessary for all the operations of reason. (369)

57. As I am writing down my thought, it escapes me sometimes, but that makes me remember my weakness, that I keep forgetting all the time; this recognition is as instructive as the thought I had forgotten, for I tend only to know my nothingness. (372)

[4] **M. de Roannez**—the Duke de Roannez and his family were close friends of Pascal.

[5] **Spongia solis**—literally "sun sponge." Frequently interpreted as sunspots, presaging the eventual extinction of the sun. But this name was given in 1604 by Casciarolo to a stone found to be luminous in the dark. This discovery brought into question traditional views concerning the physics of light.

58. How difficult it is to propose something to the judgment of another, without influencing his judgment by the way you present it to him! If you say, "I think it beautiful," "I find it obscure," or anything else of that sort, you predispose the imagination to that judgment, or you irritate it to the contrary judgment. It is better to say nothing, and then he judges according to what he is, or rather according to what he is at the moment, and according to the atmosphere created by the other circumstances of the moment which are outside our power. But at least we shall have added nothing to these influences, unless our silence produces also its effect, depending on the significance and interpretation that his mood may give to it, or depending on what he conjectures from the movements and expression of our countenance, or the tone of our voice, if he has some skill in reading physiognomies. How difficult it is not to upset a judgment from its natural balance, or rather how few judgments are really firm and stable! (105)

59. *Skepticism*—Each thing is here true in part, false in part. Truth in its essence is not thus: it is completely pure and completely true. This mixture dishonors it and destroys it. Nothing is purely true; and thus nothing is true in the strict sense of pure truth. You will say that it is true that homicide is evil; yes, for we are quite familiar with evil and falsity. But what will you say is good? Chastity? I say not, for human life would cease. Marriage? No; continence is better. Not to kill? No, for the resulting disorders would be horrible, and the wicked would kill all the good. To kill? No, for that destroys nature. We have the true and the good only in part, and mixed with the evil and the false. (385)

60. I can well conceive a man without hands, feet, head (for it is only experience that teaches us that the head is more necessary than the feet). But I cannot conceive a

man without thought; he would be a stone or a brute. (339)

61. Thought makes the greatness of man. (346)

62. If an animal did by intelligence what it does by instinct, and if it expressed through intelligence what it expresses through instinct in hunting, and to inform its fellows that the prey is found or lost, it would certainly speak also for things in which it is more deeply concerned, as to say: "Gnaw away this cord which is hurting me, and which I cannot reach." (342)

computer

63. The calculating machine produces results which come closer to thought than anything that animals do; but it does nothing which can make us say of it that it has a will, as animals do. (340)

64. *Thought*—All man's dignity is in thought. But what is that thought? How stupid it is!

Thought is then an admirable thing and by its nature beyond compare. It would have to have strange defects for it to be an object of scorn, but it has such great ones that nothing is more ridiculous. How great it is by its nature! How low it is by its faults! (365)

65. Man is but a reed, the weakest in nature, but he is a thinking reed. The whole universe need not arm itself to crush him; a vapor, a drop of water is enough to kill him. But even though the universe should crush him, man would still be nobler than what kills him since he knows that he dies, and the advantage that the universe has over him; the universe knows nothing of it.

All our dignity consists then in thought. It is upon thought that we must raise ourselves up, and not on space and time which we cannot fill. Let us strive then to think well; that is the foundation of all morality. (347)

66. *Thinking reed*—It is not from space that I must seek my dignity, but it is from the ordering of my thought. The possession of lands would give me nothing more. By space, the universe envelops me and swallows me up like a point. By thought, I envelop it. (348)

67. Reason commands us more imperiously than a master. By disobeying one we are unhappy, and by disobeying the other we are foolish. (345)

68. The truth is so obscured in our day, and falsehood so firmly established, that unless one loves the truth one cannot even know it. (864)

69. Clever people are those who know the truth, but who support it only so far as their own interest coincides with it. Beyond that, they abandon it. (583)

70. Continual reversal of the pro and the con.

We have shown, then, that man is vain by the esteem in which he holds things which are not essential; and all such opinions are thereby destroyed. We have shown next that all these opinions are quite sound and that thus, all these vanities being very well founded, the people are less vain than is supposed; and thus we have destroyed the opinion which destroyed the popular one.

But we must destroy now this last proposition, and show that it still remains true that the people are vain, although their opinions are sound; because they do not feel the truth where it is; and because, putting the truth where it is not, their opinions are always quite false and most unsound. (328)

SECTION E—MAN'S NATURE

71. Fathers fear that the natural love children bear their parents may fade away. What is then this nature,

subject to fading away? Custom is a second nature, which destroys the first one. But what is nature? Why is custom not natural? I greatly fear that nature may in itself be but a first custom, as custom is a second nature. (93)

72. The nature of man is completely natural, thoroughly animal. There is nothing that he cannot make natural to him; there is nothing natural that cannot be taken away from him. (94)

73. When we are accustomed to using bad reasons to prove the effects of nature, we no longer consent to accepting good ones when they are discovered. One might cite as an example the circulation of the blood to explain why the vein swells beneath the ligature. (96)

74. *Prejudice leading to error*—It is a deplorable thing to see all men deliberate only about means, and not about the end. Each thinks how he will conduct himself in the position he occupies; but as for the choice of position, and of fatherland, fate decides it for him.

It is a pitiful thing to see so many Turks, heretics, infidels, follow the way of life of their fathers, for this sole reason that each has been prejudiced to believe that it is the best. And that is what assigns each to his place as locksmith, soldier, etc.

That is why savages are unconcerned about Provence. (98)

75. The most important thing in all life is the choice of a profession; chance determines it. Custom makes masons, soldiers, roofers. "He is an excellent roofer," they say; and, speaking of soldiers, "They are great fools"; and others on the contrary say, "There is nothing so great as war; the rest of men are worthless." By dint of hearing in childhood these professions praised, and all others scorned, one makes his choice, for naturally people love worth and hate folly. These words in themselves will bring the decision—

the only error is in the application of the principle. So great is the force of custom that from those whom nature has formed only as men one draws all the ranks and conditions of mankind; for certain regions produce nothing but masons, others soldiers, etc. Doubtless nature is not so uniform. It is custom, then, which brings that about, for it constrains nature; and sometimes nature overcomes custom, and holds man to his instinct, in spite of all custom, good or bad. (97)

76. Nature always keeps repeating the same things— years, days, hours; spaces, too, and numbers are in succession one after the other. Thus is formed a sort of infinity and eternity. It is not that there is in all that anything truly infinite and eternal, but these finite things are multiplied infinitely. Thus it seems to me that there is only the number which multiplies them which is infinite. (121)

77. *Contradictions*—Man is naturally credulous, incredulous, timid, rash. (125)

78. Man's condition: inconstancy, boredom, anxiety. (127)

79. Description of man: dependence, desire for independence, need. (126)

80. "He lit the earth by a lamp."[6] There is little connection between the weather and my mood. I have my fogs and my fine weather within me; the success or the failure of my affairs have little to do with it. I strive readily sometimes against misfortune; the glory of conquering it makes me conquer it gaily; on the contrary, I am sometimes depressed in the midst of good fortune. (107)

[6] lamp—a reference to Montaigne's "Apology of Raymond Sebond," where Cicero is quoted in an adaptation of two lines from the *Odyssey* [XVIII, 135] on th subect of this thought.

81. Our ˙nature is in movement; complete repose is death. (129)

82. *Ennui*—Nothing is so unbearable to man as to be in a complete repose, without passions, without business, without amusement, without application. He feels then his nothingness, his abandonment, his inadequacy, his dependence, his impotence, his emptiness. Straightway there will rise from the depths of his soul boredom, gloom, sadness, grief, anger, irritation, despair. (131)

83. *Agitation*—When a soldier complains of the trouble he has, or a plowman, etc., just place them in a situation where they have nothing to do. (130)

84. Only the combat pleases us, but not the victory; we like to see combats between animals, but not the victor finishing off the vanquished. What did we want to see, if not the end of the victory? And as soon as it arrives, we are sick of it. It is the same in games, as well as in the pursuit of truth. We like to see, in debates, the conflict of opinions, but to contemplate the truth once it is found, not at all. For truth to be noted with pleasure, we must see it born out of the dispute. Similarly, in passions, there is pleasure in seeing two contraries clash; but when one is completely dominant, it then becomes only a matter of brutality. We never seek things, but only the pursuit of things. Thus in dramas peaceful scenes without fear are not good, nor are extreme miseries without hope, nor brutal loves, nor harsh severities. (135)

85. *Diversion*—When I have set myself sometimes to considering the various agitations of men, and the perils and troubles to which they expose themselves at court or in war, from which arise so many quarrels, passions, bold and often evil enterprises, etc., I have concluded that the whole misfortune of men comes from a single thing, and that is their inability to remain at rest in a room. A man

who has enough wealth to live on, if he could remain at home with pleasure, would not leave it to go to sea or to the siege of a fortified place. Men will pay so much for a military commission only because they would find it unendurable not to stir from the city; and people seek social intercourse and the diversion of gambling only because they cannot remain home with pleasure.

But when I examined the problem more closely, and after finding the cause of all our misfortunes I sought to discover the underlying reason, I found that there is a most effective one which consists in the natural misfortune of our weak and mortal condition, so wretched that nothing can console us when we think of it with close attention.

Whatever social rank we may imagine, if we bring together all the good things which can belong to us, kingship is the finest position in the world. Let us however imagine a king, sharing all the satisfactions that are inherent in his state. If he is without diversion, and if he is permitted to reflect on what he is, that languishing felicity will not support him; he will of necessity fall to contemplating what threatens him, revolts which can arise, and ultimately disease and death, which are inevitable. In consequence, if he is without diversion, he is at once unhappy, and more unhappy than the least of his subjects, who gambles and has a good time.

That is why gambling and the company of women, war, high positions, are so much sought after. It is not that in them lies indeed happiness, nor that one imagines that true bliss is to have the money he can win gambling, or in the hare that he is hunting. He would not want that hare if it were offered to him. It is not that soft and peaceful satisfaction (a state which lets us think of our wretched condition) which we seek, nor the dangers of war, nor the woes of high position, but it is the hurly-burly which turns us aside from thinking about our lot and which diverts us.

That is why men are so fond of noise and excitement; that is why prison is so horrible a torment; that is why the pleasure of solitude is an incomprehensible thing. And this is after all the greatest source of happiness in the lot of kings, that people unceasingly seek to divert them and to procure for them all kinds of pleasures.

The king is surrounded by people whose sole concern is to divert him, and to prevent him from thinking of himself. For he is unhappy, king though he be, if he thinks of that.

That is what men have been able to invent to make themselves happy. And those who philosophize about that, and who consider that people are most unreasonable to spend a whole day running after a hare that they would never wish to buy, scarcely know human nature. That hare would not protect us from the spectacle of death and of our miseries, but hunting—which turns us away from it—does protect us from it.

And thus, when they are told as a reproach that what they seek with so much ardor could not satisfy them, if they answered, as they ought to if they thought carefully about it, that they are seeking thereby only a violent and impetuous occupation which turns them aside from thinking of themselves, and that it is for that reason that they seek to attain an attractive object which charms and lures them ardently, they would leave their adversaries without an answer. But they do not answer thus, because they do not know themselves. They do not know that it is only the hunt, and not the prize, that they value.

They imagine that, if they had obtained that post, they would rest afterwards with pleasure; but they do not recognize the insatiable nature of their desire. They believe that they are sincerely seeking repose, and in reality they seek only agitation.

They have a secret instinct which drives them to seek diversion and occupation outside themselves, an instinct which rises from the feeling of their never-ending miseries; and they have another secret instinct, which derives from the greatness of our original nature, which makes them know that happiness is indeed only in repose, and not in tumult. Out of these two contrary instincts, there is formed in them a confused project, which is hidden from their sight in the depths of their soul, which prompts them to seek repose through agitation, and to imagine always that the satisfaction which they do not possess will come to them if, by surmounting a few difficulties which they envisage, they can thus open for themselves the door to repose.

Thus all of life is spent. We seek rest through overcoming a few obstacles; and if we have surmounted them, rest becomes unendurable, for either we think of the troubles we have had, or of those which threaten us. And even though one should find himself fairly well protected on all sides, boredom, all on its own, would not fail to rise from the depths of the heart, where it has its natural roots, and to fill the mind with its venom.

Thus man is so unhappy that he would grow bored, even without any cause of boredom, by the very nature of his moral being; and he is so illogical that, being full of a thousand essential causes for boredom, the slightest thing, a billiard cue and a ball that he strikes, for example, are sufficient to divert him.

But, you will say, what goal does he pursue in all that? That of boasting tomorrow among his friends that he played better than someone else. Similarly, others sweat in their studies to prove to scholars that they have solved a problem in algebra hitherto unanswerable; and so many others expose themselves to the utmost perils in order to boast afterwards about a stronghold which they have captured, and just as stupidly, in my opinion; and finally others kill themselves in their effort to take note of all these things, not in order to grow wiser because of it, but only to show that they know them, and these are the most stupid of the lot, since they are stupid with knowledge, while one might think of the others that they would no longer be stupid if they had that knowledge.

A certain man passes his life without boredom by gambling each day a trifling sum. Give him each morning what he can win during the day, on condition that he not gam-

ble, and you make him unhappy. You will say perhaps
that it is because he seeks the amusement of gambling,
and not the winnings. Have him play for nothing; he will
not grow excited, and will be bored at it. It is not, then,
the mere amusement he seeks; amusement, if languishing
and passionless, will bore him. He must grow excited at it
and must delude himself, imagining that he would be
happy to win what he would not want to receive as a gift
on condition that he not gamble, so that he may create for
himself something to grow excited about, and so that he
may stimulate on account of it his desire, his anger, his
fear, as children who take fright at the face which they
have crudely drawn.

How does it happen that this man, who lost a few
months ago his only son, and who, crushed beneath a
burden of lawsuits and disputes, was this morning so trou-
bled, is no longer concerned about his woes? Do not be
astonished; he is completely occupied in seeing where this
wild boar will pass that his dogs have been pursuing with
so much ardor for six hours. That is all it takes. Man,
however full of sadness he may be, if he can be prevailed
upon to enter into some diversion, becomes happy for the
time being; and man, however happy he may be, if he is
not diverted and occupied by some passion or some amusement which prevents boredom from spreading, will soon
be moody and unhappy. Without diversion, there is no
joy; with diversion, there is no sadness. And this is also
what forms the happiness of persons of high rank, the fact
that they have a number of people who divert them and
that they have the power to maintain themselves in that
state.

Take care! What else is it to be finance minister, chancellor, presiding justice, if not to be in a condition where one
has from early morning a great number of people who
come from all directions so that not an hour in the day is
left for them to think of themselves. And when they are in
disgrace and banished to their country homes, where they

lack neither possessions, nor servants to assist them in their
needs, they do not fail to feel wretched and abandoned,
because no one prevents them from thinking of
themselves. (139)

86. *Diversion*—Is not the dignity of the kingship great
enough in itself for him who possesses it to be made happy
at the mere sight of what he is? Will it be necessary to
divert him from that thought as in the case of ordinary
people? I realize that it is making a man happy to divert
him from the spectacle of his private misfortune to fill all
his thoughts with the painstaking effort to dance well. But
will the same hold true for a king, and will he be happier
by fixing his attention upon these vain amusements rather
than upon the spectacle of his greatness? And what object
more satisfying could one propose to his attention? Would
it not be detrimental to his joy to concern his mind with
thinking about timing his steps to the cadence of a musical
air, or about serving a tennis ball skillfully, instead of
letting him enjoy at rest the contemplation of the majestic
glory which surrounds him? Just put the matter to a test;
leave a king all alone, without any satisfaction of the
senses, without anything to occupy his mind, without company, to think at full leisure about himself, and you will
see that a king without diversion is a man full of miseries.
And so one avoids that with great care, and there never
fail to be about the persons of kings a great number of
people whose task it is to make diversion follow business,
and who observe every moment of their leisure in order to
furnish them pleasures and games so that there may be no
empty minutes; in other words, kings are surrounded by
persons who are marvelously attentive to take care that the
king is never alone and in a position to think of himself,
knowing well that he will be miserable, however much a
king he be, if he thinks of that.

I am not speaking in all this of Christian kings as Christians, but simply as kings. (142)

87. *Diversion*—Men are taught from childhood to take care of their honor, their fortune, their friends, and even the fortune and honor of their friends. They are overwhelmed with tasks to perform, the required training in languages and exercises, and they are informed that they cannot be happy unless their health, their honor, their fortune and that of their friends, are carefully preserved, and that a single thing which might be missing would make them unhappy. Thus they are given burdens and tasks which drive them constantly from daybreak on. "That," you will say, "is a strange way to make them happy! What could be done more likely to make them unhappy?" What are you saying? What could one do? One would have only to take from them all these cares, for then they would see themselves, they would think of what they are, whence they come, and where they are going; and for this reason one cannot do too much to keep them occupied and to turn them away from such ideas. And that is why, after preparing so much for them to do, if they have a little free time, one advises them to use it in amusing themselves, in playing, and in remaining even then completely occupied.

How hollow is the human heart, and how full of corruption! (143)

88. *Diversion*—Men not having been able to cure death, misery, ignorance, they have taken it into their heads, in order to make themselves happy, not to think of them. (168)

89. In spite of these miseries, he wants to be happy, and wants only to be happy, and cannot not wish to be so. But how shall he go about it? It would be necessary, in order to do it properly, that he make himself immortal; but, not being able to do that, he has decided to prevent himself from thinking of death. (169)

90. *Diversion*—If man were happy, he would be all the happier as he were less diverted, like the saints and God. —Yes, but is it not being happy to be able to find pleasure in diversion?—No, for it comes from elsewhere and from outside; and thus it is dependent, and therefore subject to being disturbed by a thousand accidents, and that makes afflictions inevitable. (170)

91. The only thing which consoles us for our miseries is diversion, and yet it is the greatest of our miseries. For that is what prevents us principally from thinking about ourselves, and which, without our being aware of it, brings about our ruin. Were it not for that, we should be plunged in boredom, and that boredom would drive us to seek a more solid means of emerging from it. But diversion amuses us, and permits us insensibly to reach the end of life's journey. (171)

92. We know ourselves so little that many think they are going to die when they are in good health; others think they are in good health when they are close to death, not perceiving the approaching fever, or the abscess ready to form. (175)

93. Cromwell was set to ravage the whole of Christendom; the royal family would have been ruined, and his own forever powerful, had it not been for a little grain of sand which lodged in his ureter. Even Rome was ready to tremble before him, but that bit of gravel having lodged there, he died, his family toppled, everything returned to peace, and the king was set on his throne again. (176)

94. Great and small, men are subject to the same accidents, the same annoyances, and the same passions; but one man is at the top of the wheel, and the other near the center, and the latter is thus less agitated by the same movements. (180)

95. We run heedlessly over the edge of the precipice, after placing something before our eyes to keep ourselves from seeing it. (183)

96. Man's nature may be considered from two different viewpoints: one, according to his destined end, and then he is great and incomparable; the other, according to the common run of men, as one judges the nature of the horse and the dog by the common run, seeing in them their speed and their spirit of alertness, and then man is abject and vile. And those are the two approaches which lead to such contradictory judgments, and which cause so many disputes among philosophers.

For one denies the supposition of the other. One says, "He was not born for that destiny, for all his actions contradict it." The other says, "He departs from his destiny when he does those base actions." (415)

97. Man's greatness is great in that he knows himself wretched. A tree does not know itself wretched.

It is then being wretched to know oneself wretched; but it is being great to know that one is wretched. (397)

98. *Man's greatness*—Man's greatness is so obvious that it can be seen even in his misery. For what is nature for animals, we call it misery in man; thus we recognize that his nature being today like that of animals, he has fallen from a better nature which was formerly peculiar to him.

For who is unhappy at not being king, except a dispossessed king? Did anyone consider L. Aemilius Paulus[7] unhappy because he was no longer consul? On the contrary, everyone thought that he was fortunate for having been consul, because his condition was not to be so forever. But people considered Perseus[8] so unfortunate to be no longer

[7] **Paulus**—Roman general; consul 182 and 168 B.C.

[8] **Perseus**—last king of Macedon (179-168 B.C.); defeated by L. Aemilius Paulus.

king, because his condition was to be so always, that they thought it strange that he should continue to endure life. Who considers himself unfortunate that he has only one mouth? And who would not consider himself unfortunate to have only one eye? No one has perhaps ever thought of bemoaning his fate for not having three eyes, but one is inconsolable for having none at all. (409)

99. All those miseries themselves prove his greatness. They are miseries of a great lord, miseries of a dispossessed king. (398)

100. Man knows not in what rank to place himself. He is obviously out of his element, and fallen from his true place without being able to find it again. He seeks it everywhere with anxiety and without success amid impenetrable darkness. (427)

101. We wish truth, and we find only uncertainty.

We seek happiness, and we find only misery and death.

We are incapable of not wishing for truth and happiness, and are incapable of either certitude or happiness. This desire is left to us as much to punish us as to make us feel from where we are fallen. (437)

102. War within man between reason and passions.

If he had only reason without passions . . .

If he had only passions without reason . . .

But having both, he cannot be without war, not being able to have peace with one except by having war with the other. Thus he is always divided and contrary to himself. (412)

103. This inner war of reason against passions has resulted in a division into two sects among those who have sought to find peace. Some have endeavored to renounce passions and to become gods; others have endeavored

(like Des Barreaux[9]) to renounce reason and become mere brutes. But they have not succeeded, on either side; reason always remains, accusing the baseness and injustice of the passions, and disturbing the repose of those who abandon themselves to them; and the passions are still alive within those who seek to renounce them. (413)

104. Man's nature is not to advance at an even pace; it has its moments of advance and of retreat.

Fever has its alternance or chills and burning heat, and the chill reveals the magnitude of the fever's burning just as much as the heat itself does.

The inventions of men from century to century proceed in the same way. It is the same with the goodness and maliciousness of the world in general: "Often changes are most pleasing even to the great." [10] (354)

105. Continuous eloquence is wearisome.

Princes and kings sometimes play. They are not always on their thrones; they grow bored there—greatness must be put aside in order to be appreciated. Continuity is distasteful in everything; cold is welcome because of the pleasure of warming oneself.

Nature acts by progression, advancing by degrees. It passes and returns, then goes farther, then only half as far, then more than ever, etc.

The ebb and flow of the sea occur in this fashion; the sun seems to advance in this way. (355)

106. He who does not see the vanity of the world is very vain himself. And so who does not see it, except young people who are completely occupied with excitement, amusement, and thoughts of the future? But take away their diversions, you will see them wither with boredom. They feel then their nothingness, without recognizing

---

[9] Des Barreaux—French poet (1602-1673); a famous atheist ultimately converted to Christianity.

[10] Horace, *Odes* III, xxix, 13.

it, for it is to be wretched to be in an unendurable sadness as soon as one is reduced to considering himself and not having his thought turned aside from that consideration. (164)

107.   The last act is bloody, however beautiful the drama may be in all its other parts; they finally throw some earth over your head, and it is all over for ever. (210)

108. I blame equally those who make it a policy to praise man, and those who make it a policy to blame him, and those who set out to seek diversion. I can approve only those who seek in the midst of tears. (421)

109. One does not grow bored with eating and sleeping every day, for hunger is reborn, and drowsiness; otherwise one would grow weary of them. Thus without the hunger for spiritual things one would grow weary of them. Hunger for justice—eighth beatitude. (264)

110. In spite of the sight of all our miseries, which touch us, which grip us by the throat, we have an instinct which we cannot repress and which lifts us up. (411)

111. Those great spiritual efforts of which the soul is sometimes capable are not something it can long maintain. It leaps up to them merely, not as one sits upon a throne for all time, but just for a fleeting moment. (351)

SECTION F—OBSERVATIONS ON MAN IN SOCIETY

112. The wisecracker—a malicious character. (46)

113. Do you wish people to think well of you?—Do not praise yourself. (44)

114. The more intelligence a person has, the more men of originality he recognizes. Common people do not recognize any difference between men. (7)

115. We must have pity for one another; but we must feel for some a pity born of tenderness and, for others, a pity born of disdain. (194 *bis*)

116. Two kinds of people fail to recognize any difference between things, as between holy days and working days, Christians and priests, one sin and another. And as a consequence one group concludes that what is therefore wrong for priests is wrong also for all Christians; and the other group that what is not wrong for Christians is permissible for priests. (866)

117. *Montaigne*—The faults of Montaigne are great. Lascivious expressions; their use has no value, in spite of Mademoiselle de Gournay.[11] Credulous: *people without eyes*. Ignorant: *squaring of the circle, greater world*. His views on voluntary suicide, on death. He inspires an indifference toward salvation, *without fear and without repentance*. Since the purpose of his book was not to incline his reader toward piety, he was under no obligation to do so; but the writer is always under an obligation not to turn his reader away from piety. We may excuse his somewhat free and voluptuous feelings in certain situations life presents, but we cannot excuse his completely pagan attitude toward death; for one must renounce all piety if one does not at least wish to die as a good Christian. Now throughout his whole book he contemplates death only as a coward and a weakling. (63)

118. Two simliar countenances, neither of which would make us laugh by itself, make us laugh when we see them together because of their resemblance. (133)

---

[11] **Mlle. de Gournay**—adoptive daughter and literary executor of Montaigne. She prepared the posthumous edition or the *Essays* of 1595.

119. What an empty thing is that sort of painting which attracts admiration by its resemblance to things when the originals of those things are in no way admirable. (134)

120. I maintain that if all men knew what they say about one another, there would not be four friends in the world. That is evident by the quarrels caused by the indiscreet reports which are sometimes made concerning what has been said. (101)

121. A true friend is such an advantageous thing, even for the greatest lords, so that he may speak well of them and support them even in their absence, that they must do everything possible to have such friends. But let them choose well; for if they put forth all their efforts on behalf of fools, that will be useless to them, whatever good those fools may say about them. And, indeed, fools will not say good about them when there is need to defend them vigorously, for they lack authority; and thus they will say evil about them in company. (155)

122. Whoever would wish to know fully the vanity of man has only to consider the causes and effects of love. The cause is an *I know not what* (Corneille), and its effects are frightening. This indefinable something, this thing so slight that one cannot recognize it, moves the earth, princes, armies, the whole world.

Cleopatra's nose: had it been shorter, the whole face of the earth would be different. (162)

123. All great diversions are dangerous for Christian life, but among all those which society has invented there is none which is more to be feared than the theater. It offers so natural and so delicate a representation of the passions that it arouses them and makes them come alive within our heart, and especially the passion of love. This is all the more true when it is depicted as most chaste and most respectable. For the more innocent it appears to inno-

cent souls, the more susceptible are they of being touched by it. Its violence pleases our ego, which straightway conceives the desire to cause the same effects we have just seen so well portrayed; and at the same time our judgment is conditioned by the respectability of the sentiments seen in the play; and thus pure souls lose their timidity, and they imagine that there is no offense against purity in loving with a love which seems to them so reasonable.

Thus we leave the theater with our hearts so full of all the beauties and all the sweetness of love, and with the soul and mind convinced of our innocence, that we are quite ready to feel love's first impressions, or rather to seek the opportunity to arouse them in someone's heart in order to experience the same pleasures and the same sacrifices as we have seen so well depicted in the play. (11)

124. Man is obviously made for thought; that is all his dignity and all his merit, and his whole duty is to think properly. Now the order of thought is to begin with oneself, and with one's creator, and one's end.

Now what do people think of? Never of these things, but of dancing, playing the lute, singing, writing verses, riding at rings, dueling, becoming king—without thinking of what it is to be king, and what it is to be a man. (146)

125. *Mine, thine*—"This dog is mine," say these poor children; "That is my place in the sun."—That is the beginning and the image of all usurpation on this earth. (295)

126. The greatest pettiness for man is the pursuit of glory, but it is that very pursuit which is the greatest mark of his excellence; for whatever he may possess on earth, whatever health and essential comfort he may have, he is not satisfied unless he is held in esteem by men. He has such regard for man's reason that, whatever advantage he may have on earth, if he does not occupy also an advanta-

geous place in man's reason he is not happy. That is the finest distinction in the world; nothing can turn him away from this desire, and that is the most persistent quality of the human heart.

And those who despise men most, and reduce them to the level of beasts, still want to be admired and believed, and contradict themselves by their own feeling; their nature, which is stronger than anything, convinces them of the greatness of man more strongly than reason convinces them of their pettiness. (404)

127. *Glory*—Animals do not admire one another. A horse does not admire his stablemate. It is not that there is among them no rivalry in racing, but that is without consequence, for once back at the stable the heavier and less gracefully built one does not for that reason yield his share of oats to the other, as men wish to have others do to them. Their worth is satisfied with itself. (401)

128. *Man's greatness*—We have so great an idea of man's soul that we cannot endure being despised by it, and not being held in the esteem of a soul; and all men's felicity consists in this esteem. (400)

129. The bonds that attach the respect of some toward others are, in general, bonds of necessity; for there must be different degrees, all men wishing to dominate, and all not being able to do so, but some being capable of it.

Let us imagine, then, that we see those bonds beginning to form. It is certain that men will fight until the stronger part oppresses the weaker, and until finally there is a dominant party. But when that is once determined, then the masters, who do not want war to continue, order that the force which they now hold will pass to others as they wish; some leave it up to the choice of the people, others to succession by right of birth, etc.

And that is where imagination begins to play its rôle.

Up to that point, pure force prevails; now it is force which is vested by the imagination in a certain party, in France the aristocracy, and in Switzerland the commoners, etc.

Now those bonds which thus attach respect to this or that person in particular are bonds of imagination. (304)

130. As duchies and kingships and magistrateships are real and necessary because of the fact that force rules everything, they are to be found in all places and at all times. But because it is only caprice which puts this person or that into such a position, that is not constant, that is subject to change. (306)

131. The Swiss are offended at being called noblemen, and prove their origin as commoners in order to be judged worthy of high office. (305)

132. The chancellor is grave and covered with ornaments, for his position is false. Not so the king: he does have power, so he has nothing to do with imagination. Judges, physicians, etc. have only imagination. (307)

133. The habit of seeing kings accompanied by guards, drummers, officers, and all the things which incline us physically toward respect and terror, brings it about that their countenance, when they are sometimes alone and without these accompanying personages, impresses upon their subjects respect and terror, because in thought we do not separate their persons from their followers whom we usually see joined with them. And people, not realizing that this effect results from that habit, believe that it comes from a natural force. For that reason we hear such remarks as: "The character of divinity is imprinted upon his countenance, etc." (308)

134. *Sound opinions of the people*—The greatest of evils is civil war. Civil wars are certain if one wishes to reward merits, for all will say that they are deserving. The

harm to be feared from a fool who succeeds by right of birth is neither so great nor so certain. (313)

135. The power of kings is founded upon the reason and the folly of the people, and to a far greater degree upon their folly. The greatest and most important thing in the world has for its foundation weakness, and that foundation is admirably sure, for there is nothing more certain than that the people will be weak. What is founded upon sound reason is quite ill founded, as is the esteem of wisdom. (330)

136. Have you never seen persons who, to complain about the slight attention you pay them, set forth for you the example of people of high rank who hold them in esteem? I should answer them thus: "Show me the merit by which you have charmed those persons, and I shall esteem you similarly." (333)

137. How right we are to distinguish men by their exterior, rather than by inner qualities! Which one of us two will pass first? Which one will yield his place to the other? The less clever? But I am as clever as he; we will have to fight over that. He has four lackeys, and I have only one; that is visible, you have only to count, it is up to me to yield, and I am a fool if I contest it. Here we are at peace by this device, and that is the greatest of benefits. (319)

138. One imagines Plato and Aristotle only clothed in the full robes of a pedant. They were worthy men and, like others, good company in the presence of their friends. And when they amused themselves writing their *Laws* and their *Politics,* they did so for amusement; it was the least philosophic and the least serious part of their lives—the most philosophic was to live simply and quietly. If they wrote on politics, it was as it were to regulate an insane asylum; and if they pretended to speak of it as of a great thing, it is because they knew that the fools to whom they

were speaking thought they were emperors and kings. They accept their principles in order to moderate their folly to the least harmful degree possible. (331)

139. *Skepticism*—Too keen intelligence is accused of madness, as is too great a lack of it. Nothing but mediocrity is good. It is the majority that has established that, and that snaps at whoever goes beyond mediocrity at either end. I will not be obstinate, and I accept being thus classified. I will not let myself be at the low end, not because it is low, but because it is an end, for I should refuse similarly to be placed at the top. It means leaving the ranks of humanity if one leaves the middle range. The greatness of the human soul consists in knowing how to keep its place there; greatness does not reside in leaving humanity behind, but quite to the contrary in not leaving it. (378)

SECTION G—MORAL VALUES AND JUSTICE

140. Never does one do evil so fully and so gaily as when one does it as a matter of conscience. (895)

141. All good maxims are current in society; men simply fail to apply them. For example, they do not doubt that one must risk one's life to defend the public good, but they do not do it for religion.

It is necessary that there be inequality among men, that is true; but, that being granted, there is the door open, not only to the highest domination, but to the highest tyranny.

It is necessary that the spirit not be completely uncompromising; but that opens the door to the greatest excesses. Set limits beyond which one must not go. But there are no limits in things; the laws seek to impose limits, and the spirit cannot abide them. (380)

142. By knowing the dominant passion of each man, one is sure of pleasing him; and yet each has his fantasies,

contrary to his own good, in the very idea he has of the good. That is a peculiarity which makes general rules inapplicable. (106)

143. When everything is moving in the same direction and at the same speed, nothing seems to be moving, as aboard a ship. When all are moving precipitously toward excesses, none seems to be so moving. He who stops makes the mad rush of the others perceptible, as would a fixed point. (382)

144. Those who live in disorder say to those who live in order that they are the ones who are deviating from nature; and they believe that they are following nature themselves, as those who are aboard a ship believe that those who are on the shore are moving away. On all sides, people say the same thing. One must have a fixed point in order to judge movement. The port permits judging those who are aboard a ship, but where shall we find a port in matters of morality? (383)

145. Good deeds kept hidden are the most to be esteemed. When I encounter some in history, as page 184,[12] they please me greatly. But after all, they have not been completely hidden, since they have been known; and although one did everything possible to conceal them, this trifle which permitted them to appear spoils everything; but that is the finest thing, to have sought to conceal them. (159)

146. *Glory*—Admiration spoils everything from earliest childhood. "Oh! How well expressed that is! Oh! How well he did! How good he is!" Etc.

The children of Port-Royal, from whom this spur of envy and glory is withheld, fall into indifference. (151)

[12] Montaigne I, 14; examples of the wife of Sabinus and of two Spartan boys.

147.　. . . on what will he base the constitution of the society which he seeks to govern? Will it be upon the whim of each individual? What confusion! Will it be upon justice? Society does not know what it is.

Certainly, if society knew it, it would not have established this maxim, the most general of all those which exist among men, that each should follow the custom of his country; the light of true equity would have been accepted by all peoples; and legislators would not have taken as a model, instead of that constant justice, the fantasies and caprices of the Persians and the Germans. One would see justice established in all the states of the world and in all times, whereas we see nothing just or unjust which does not change quality with a change of climate. Three degrees of distance from the pole change completely the whole system of jurisprudence; a meridian determines the truth; in but a few years of possession, constitutional laws change; law has its periodic phases; the entrance of Saturn into the constellation Leo marks for us the origin of a certain crime. Amusing justice that changes with the crossing of a river! Truth on this side of the Pyrenees, error beyond.

They confess that justice is not in these customs, but that it resides in the natural laws, common to all countries. Certainly they would defend it stubbornly, if in the rashness of the chance which sowed human laws there had been encountered a single one which was universal; but the amusing thing is that the caprice of men is so diversified that there is no universal law at all.

Larceny, incest, the murder of children and parents, all have had their place among virtuous actions. Can there be anything more amusing than that a man should have the right to kill me because he lives across the water, and because his prince has a quarrel against mine, although I have none with him?

There are doubtless natural laws, but this fine corrupted reason of ours has corrupted everything. "Nothing remains that is ours; what we call ours is a product of convention." [13] "Crimes are committed as a consequence of decrees of the senate and plebiscites." [14] "We used to suffer from our vices; today we suffer from our laws." [15]

Out of this confusion there results that one person says that the essence of justice is the authority of the legislator; another, that it is the good pleasure of the sovereign; another, that it is present custom, and this is the most sure. Nothing, according to reason alone, is just in itself; everything changes with time. Custom determines all justice, for this simple reason that it is accepted; that is the mystic foundation of its authority. Whoever will trace justice back to its principle destroys it. Nothing is so faulty as those laws that correct faults; whoever obeys them because they are just, obeys the justice that he imagines, but not the essence of the law. The law is based on nothing outside itself; it is the law, and nothing more.

Whoever chooses to examine the principle of the law will find it so weak and so slight that, if he is not accustomed to contemplating the marvels of human imagination, he will be amazed that a century should have endowed it with so much pomp and reverence. The art of revolt, of overthrowing states, is to upset established customs by probing to their very source in order to reveal their lack of authority and justice. One must, they say, return to the fundamental and original laws of the state that an unjust custom has abolished. It is a device sure to ruin everything; nothing will be just weighed in that balance. And yet the people readily listen to these speeches. They shake off the yoke as soon as they recognize it; and men of high rank take advantage of this for the greater misfortune of the people, and of those curious seekers after the origins of established customs. That is why the wisest lawgiver[16] was wont to say that, for their own good, one must often deceive men; and another, a

[13] Cicero, *On Ends* V, 21.
[14] Seneca, *Epistles* XCV.
[15] Tacitus, *Annals* III, 25.
[16] Plato.

good expert in politics, declared: "As he is ignorant of the truth which frees, it is good that he should be deceived." [17] The people must not feel the truth of the usurpation; it was introduced long ago without reason, and it has become reasonable; it is essential that it be looked upon as authentic and eternal, and that its source be hidden, if one does not wish it soon to come to an end. (294)

148. Why do you kill me?—Well! Do you not live on the other side of the water? My friend, if you lived on this side I should be an assassin, and it would be unjust to kill you this way; but since you live on the other side, I am a hero and my action is just. (293)

149. When it is a question of judging whether one should go to war and kill so many men, condemn so many Spaniards to death, it is one man who makes the decision, and an interested party at that; it ought to be a third party not involved in the dispute. (296)

150. Justice is what is established; and thus all established laws will necessarily be considered just without being examined, simply because they are established. (312)

151. *Justice*—As fashion determines what is pleasing, so too it determines what is just. (309)

152. I spent a great part of my life believing that there was a justice, and in that I was not mistaken, for there is one according as God has been willing to reveal it to us. But I did not consider it that way, and that is where I was wrong; for I thought that our justice was essentially just, and that I was capable of knowing it and judging it. But I found myself so often lacking in right judgment that finally I came to distrust myself, and then others. I have seen the

[17] Augustine, *City of God* IV, 27.

changeability of all countries and of all men; and thus, after many changes of judgment concerning real justice, I have realized that our nature was only a continual change, and I have no longer changed since; and if I did change, I should thereby confirm my opinion.

The skeptic Arcesilaus who returned to dogmatism again. (375)

153. Sneezing absorbs all the functions of the soul just as much as sexual intercourse does, but we do not draw from it the same conclusions against man's greatness because it is involuntary. And, although we may induce sneezing, nevertheless it is against our will that we induce it; it is not in view of the thing itself, but for another end; and thus it is not a mark of man's weakness, and of his enslavement under this action.

It is not shameful for man to succumb under pain, and it is shameful for him to succumb under pleasure. And this does not come about because pain comes to us from outside ourselves, while we seek pleasure; for we may seek pain, and succumb to it purposely, without this sort of baseness. Whence comes it, then, that it is glorious for reason to succumb under the effort of pain, and that it is shameful for it to succumb under the effort of pleasure? It is because it is not pain which tempts us and attracts us; we choose it deliberately and wish to make it dominate over us, so that we are masters of the thing, and in this way it is man who yields to himself; but in pleasure, it is man who yields to pleasure. Now only control and power bring glory, and only servitude is shameful. (160)

154. The only universal rules are the laws of the country for ordinary things, and majority opinion for others. What is the source of that practice? Inherent force. And thus it is that kings, whose strength comes from elsewhere, do not follow the majority opinion of their ministers.

Doubtless the equality of goods is just; but not being able to bring it about that force should reside in obedience to justice, one has brought it about that it is just to obey force; not being able to fortify justice, one has justified force, so that justice and force might coincide, and so that peace might prevail—and that is the sovereign good. (299)

155. Why do we follow the majority? Is it because they have greater reason? No, but they have greater force.

Why do we follow ancient laws and ancient opinions? Is it because they are sounder? No, but they are unique, and they take from us the root of diversity. (301)

156. *Justice, force*—It is just that what is just should be followed; it is necessary that what is strongest be followed. Justice without force is powerless; force without justice is tyrannical. Justice without force is contradicted, because there are always wicked people; force without justice is accused. We must then bring justice and force together, and, for that, either bring it about that what is just should be strong, or that what is strong should be just.

Justice is subject to dispute; force is readily recognizable and without dispute. Thus it has not been possible to give force to justice; because force has contradicted justice and has said that it was unjust, and has declared that it was force itself which was just. And thus, not being able to bring about that what is just should be strong, men have decided that what is strong is just. (298)

57. Montaigne is wrong; custom is to be followed only because it is custom, and not because it is reasonable and just. But the people follow it for the sole reason that they think it just. Otherwise, they would no longer follow it in spite of its being custom, for man wishes to be subject only to reason or justice. Custom, were it not for that, would pass for tyranny; but the power of reason and justice is no more tyrannical than that of the pursuit of pleasure—they are principles natural to man.

It would therefore be good that we should obey laws

and customs because they are laws. It would be good that
we should realize that there are no true and just ones to be
introduced, that we know nothing about truth and justice,
and that thus we must simply observe traditional laws;
that way we should never deviate from them. But the
people are not capable of that doctrine; and therefore,
since they believe that truth can be found, and that it
resides in laws and customs, they believe them and take
their antiquity for a proof of their truth (and not of their
mere authority without truth). Thus they obey them; but
they are likely to revolt as soon as they are shown that
laws have no worth, which can always be done for all of
them by considering them from a certain angle. (325)

158. *Injustice*—It is dangerous to tell the people that
laws are not just, for they obey them only because they
believe them to be just. That is why one must tell them at
the same time that they must obey them because they are
laws, as one must obey superiors, not because they are
just, but because they are superiors. In that way, all sedi-
tion is thereby forestalled if one can make them understand that, and understand properly what the definition of
justice is. (326)

159. What a man's virtue is capable of is not to be
measured by his exceptional efforts, but by his daily life.
(352)

160. I do not admire the high degree of a virtue, such
as valor, unless I see at the same time the high degree of
the opposite virtue, as in Epaminondas[18] who had extreme
valor and extreme kindness. For, otherwise, it is not a
matter of ascending but of falling. One does not show his
greatness by being at one extremity, but indeed by touch-
ing both at the same time, and filling all the space between. But perhaps it is only a sudden movement of the

[18] **Epaminondas**—Theban commander (420-362 B.C.). Made
of Thebes the most powerful of Grecian states.

soul from one extreme to the other, and it is never truly at more than one point, like the leaping flame? So be it; but at least that indicates agility of soul, if it does not mark its breadth. (353)

161. When we wish to pursue virtues to their farthest limits in both directions, vices appear which worm their way in imperceptibly along their imperceptible routes as we move toward the infinitely small; and other vices appear in swarms as we move toward the infinitely great, so that we are lost amid vices and no longer see the virtues. We lose perfection itself. (357)

162. We do not support ourselves in virtue by our own strength, but by the counterbalance of two opposing vices, as we remain standing between two contrary winds. Remove one of those vices, and we fall into the other. (359)

163. It is not good to be too free. It is not good to have everything we need. (379)

164. Man is neither angel nor beast, and it is his misfortune that he who seeks to play the rôle of angel acts most like a beast. (358)

Part II

THE WAGER

❧

SECTION A—AGAINST ATHEISTS AND SKEPTICS

165. There are only three sorts of people: those who serve God, having found him; those who put forth every effort to seek him, not having found him; those who live without seeking and without having found him. The first are reasonable and happy; the last are foolish and unhappy; the middle group are unhappy and reasonable. (257)

166. Atheism, sign of strength of mind, but up to a certain degree only. (225)

167. Atheists should declare only what is perfectly clear. Now it is not perfectly clear that the soul is material. (221)

168. What is it that feels pleasure within us? Is it our hand? Is it our arm? Is it our flesh? Is it our blood? You will see that it must be something immaterial. (339 *bis*)

169. I realize that I might very well not have been, for my self consists in my thought; then I who think would not have been if my mother had been killed before I was given life. Therefore I am not a necessary being. I am not eternal either, nor infinite; but I see clearly that there is in nature a being who is necessary, eternal, and infinite. (469)

170. Do you believe it is impossible that God should be infinite, without parts?—Yes.—I wish, then, to show you something infinite and indivisible; it is a point moving everywhere with infinite speed, for it is in all places and is complete in each.

Let this effect of nature, which seemed to you impossible before, make you realize that there can be others of which you are still not aware. Do not draw from your limited experience the conclusion that there is nothing left for you to know, but rather that there remains infinitely much for you to know. (231)

171. *Atheists*—What reason have they to say that one cannot rise from the dead? Which is more difficult, to be born, or to rise again? That what has never been should be, or that what has been should be again? Is it more difficult to come into being than to return to it? Habit makes one seem easy to us, the lack of habit makes the other impossible—a commonplace way of judging!

Why can a virgin not give birth? Does a hen not produce eggs without a rooster? And what distinguishes them from other eggs? And what makes us believe that the hen cannot form that germ there as well as the rooster? (222)

172. What have they to say against the resurrection and against the virgin birth? In what respect is it more difficult to produce than to reproduce a man or an animal? And if they had never seen any sort of animals, could they guess whether they are produced without matings among them? (223)

173. *Philosophers*—We are full of things which lead us to turn outwards.

Our instinct makes us feel that we must seek our happiness outside ourselves. Our passions make us turn outwards, even though objects do not present themselves to arouse them. The objects of outer reality tempt us by themselves and call us, even though we do not direct our thoughts to them. And thus it is useless for philosophers to say, "Withdraw into yourselves; there you will find your good." We do not believe them. Those who do believe them are the most empty and the greatest fools. (464)

174. The stoics say, "Withdraw into yourselves; it is there you will find your peace." And that is not true.

The others say, "Turn outside yourselves; seek happiness through diversion." And that is not true. Diseases come.

Happiness is neither outside us, nor within us. It is in God, both outside and within us. (465)

175. All their principles are true, those of the skeptics, the stoics, the atheists, etc. But their conclusions are false, because the opposite principles are true, too. (394)

176. Incomprehensible that God should be, and incomprehensible that he should not be; that the soul should coexist with the body, and that we should have no soul; that the world should be created, and that it should not be created, etc.; that original sin should be, and that it should not be. (230)

177. Ecclesiastes [VIII, 17] shows that man without God is in ignorance of everything, and in an inevitable state of unhappiness. For it is to be unhappy to will and yet be powerless. Now he wants to be happy and assured of some truth; and yet he can neither know, nor not desire to know. He cannot even doubt. (339)

178. *Second part: that man without faith can know neither the true good, nor justice*—All men seek to be happy—that is without exception. Whatever different means they may employ, they aim at the same goal. What makes some go to war, and others not, is this same desire which is in both groups, accompanied by different ideas about what constitutes happiness. They will never take the

slightest step except toward that goal. It is the motive of all actions of all men, including those who hang themselves.

And yet in all the course of time, never has anyone, without faith, arrived at that point toward which all aim unceasingly. All complain—princes and subjects, noblemen and commoners, old and young, strong and weak, learned and ignorant, healthy and ill, of all countries, all times, all ages, and all conditions.

An experience so long, so continuous, and so uniform ought indeed to persuade us of our inability to attain the good through our own efforts; but we learn little by example. It is never so completely identical that there is not some shade of difference; and that is why we hope that on this occasion our expectations may not be disappointed as they were before. And thus, the present never satisfying us, experience deceives us and, from misfortune to misfortune, leads us all the way to death, which is the eternal summit of all misfortunes.

What is it then that this avidity and this impotence cry out to us, except that there was formerly in man a real happiness; in him there remains only the totally empty mark and trace of that happiness, which he tries in vain to fill with everything that surrounds him, seeking from absent things the help he does not obtain from present ones, but finding all incapable of that help, because that infinite abyss can be filled only by something infinite and immutable, that is to say only by God himself.

God alone is his true good; and since he has turned away from him, it is a strange thing that there is nothing in nature which has not served on occasion to take his place—stars, firmament, earth, elements, plants, cabbages, leeks, animals, insects, calves, serpents, fever, plague, war, famine, vices, adultery, incest. And since he has lost the one true good, everything in its turn may seem to him to be the good, even to his own destruction, although so contrary to God, to reason, and to nature all together.

Some seek the good in authority, others in collections

and scholarship, others in pleasures. Others, who have indeed come closer to it, have considered that it is necessary that the universal good which all men desire not be in any of the particular things which can be possessed only by one person alone and that, when divided, afflict their possessor more by the lack of the part he does not have than they satisfy him by the enjoyment of that part which has been granted him. They have realized that the true good must be such that all may possess it simultaneously, without diminution and without envy, and that no one may lose it against his will. And their reason is that this desire being natural to man, since it is necessarily in all men and none can be without it, they have thus concluded . . . (425)

179. None other has recognized that man is the most excellent creature. Some who have been well aware of the reality of his excellence, have considered as cowardice and ingratitude the low feelings that men have naturally about themselves; and the others, who have well understood how real that baseness is, have condemned as ridiculous pride those feelings of greatness which are also natural to man.

"Raise your eyes toward God," say the first group; "See him whom you resemble, and who made you to worship him. You can make yourself like him; wisdom, if you are willing to follow it, will make you his equal." "Raise your heads, free men!" says Epictetus.[19] And the other say to him, "Lower your eyes toward the ground, puny worm that you are, and look at the beasts whose companion you are."

What will become of man? Will he be like God or like the beasts? What a frightful distance! What then will we be? Who does not see by all this that man has wandered away, that he has fallen from his place, that he seeks it anxiously, that he can no longer find it again? And who then will set him on the right road? The greatest men have not succeeded in doing so. (431)

[19] Epictetus—Stoic philosopher (60-140 A.D.).

180. Philosophers did not prescribe sentiments of due proportion for each of the two states.

They inspired movements of pure elevation, and that is not the state of man.

They inspired movements of pure humiliation, and that is not the state of man.

He must have movements of humiliation, not as a consequence of his nature, but of penitence; not as a constant attitude, but to permit him to rise to elevation. He must have movements of elevation, not because of his merit, but through grace, and after passing through humiliation. (525)

181. *Philosophers*—What a vain thing to cry out to a man who does not know himself that he should rise by himself to God! And what a vain thing to tell it to a man who does know himself! (509)

182. The true nature of man, his true good, and true virtue, and true religion, are things we can know only inseparably. (442)

183. The strongest arguments of the skeptics (I leave aside the lesser ones) are: that we have no certitude of the truth of these principles, except through faith and revelation, unless it be that we feel them naturally within us. Now this natural feeling is not a convincing proof of their truth since, having no reason for certitude other than faith as to whether man was created by a good God, by an evil demon, or by chance, it is therefore a matter of doubt whether these principles which have been given us are true, or false, or uncertain—all depends on their origin. Moreover, they maintain that no one has any assurance, except through faith, whether he is awake or asleep, since during sleep one believes he is awake as firmly as when he really is. He thinks he sees space, figures, movements; he feels time pass and measures it; and finally he believes he is acting as if he were awake. So that, half our life being

spent in sleep where, by our own admission, however it may seem, we have no idea of the truth, all our notions then being illusions, who knows whether this other half of life in which we think we are awake is not another sleep somewhat different from the first, and from which we awaken when we believe we fall asleep?

And who doubts that, if we dreamed in company, and if by chance the dreams happened to agree, which is ordinary enough, and if we were alone when awake, we might not believe the situation reversed? Finally, as we often dream that we are dreaming, piling up dream on dream, is not life itself only a dream, on which other dreams are grafted, and death our awakening from that dream? During the dream of life, are we any more aware of the principles of the true and the good than during natural sleep, those different thoughts which agitate us then being perhaps only illusions, like the passing of time and the vain phantoms of our dreams?

Those are the chief arguments on both sides.

I leave aside the lesser ones, such as the arguments of the skeptics against the impressions of custom, education, manners, country, and other similar things. Although these seem convincing to most ordinary men, who philosophize only on these vain foundations, they are readily blown down by the merest breath of the skeptics. Just look at their books, if you are not sufficiently convinced already of this; you will be quickly convinced, and perhaps too much so.

I come now to the single strong point of the dogmatists, which is that speaking in good faith and sincerely one cannot doubt natural principles. Against this, the skeptics oppose precisely the uncertainty of our origin, which involves that of our nature. Since the beginning of the world, the dogmatists are still seeking to answer that.

There you have mankind divided into two armed camps. Each must take sides, and align himself necessarily either with the skeptics or the dogmatists. For whoever hopes to remain neutral will be the perfect skeptic. That neutrality is the very essence of their school: whoever is not against them, is in the highest degree for them (which is for them a great advantage). They are not for themselves—they are neutral, indifferent, suspending judgment, without excepting themselves.

What then will man do in this situation? Will he doubt everything? Will he doubt whether he is pinched or burned? Will he doubt whether he doubts? Will he doubt his own existence? One cannot go that far, and I declare that there has never been a perfect and complete skeptic. Nature supports our puny reason, and prevents it from wandering that far.

Will he say, then, on the contrary, that he possesses beyond all doubt the truth, he who, in the face of even the mildest adversary, can produce no title deed to the truth and is obliged to give up?

What a chimera then is man! What a freak, what a monster, what a chaos, what a subject of contradiction, what a marvel! Judge of all things, and imbecile earthworm; possessor of the truth, and sink of uncertainty and error; glory and rubbish of the universe.

Who will disentangle this confusion? Nature refutes the skeptics, and reason refutes the dogmatists. What will become of you, then, O men who seek what your true condition is through the efforts of your natural reason? You can neither flee one of these sects, nor remain within the other.

Know then, proud creature, what a paradox you are to yourself. Be humbled, impotent reason; be still, foolish nature. Learn that man infinitely transcends man, and hear from your master your true condition of which you remain ignorant. Listen to God.

For finally, if man had never been corrupt, he would possess in his innocence both truth and happiness in full certainty; and if man had from all time been corrupt, he would have no idea of the truth nor of bliss. But, wretched creatures though we be, and more than if there had never been any greatness in our condition, we do have an idea of happiness, and cannot attain it; we do perceive an image of the truth, and possess only falsehood. We are incapable of being absolutely ignorant, and of knowing with certainty, so manifest is it that we were once in a degree of perfection from which we have unhappily fallen!

It is an astonishing thing, however, that the mystery farthest removed from our understanding, which is that of the transmission of sin, should be the thing without which we can have no knowledge at all of ourselves. For there is no doubt that there is nothing which offends our reason more than to say that the sin of the first man has made guilty those who, being so remote from that source, seem incapable of sharing in it. This transmission not only seems to us impossible, it seems to us even most unjust; for what is more contrary to the rules of our miserable justice than to damn eternally a child incapable of will, for a sin in which he seems to have so little share, for it was committed six thousand years before he came into being? Certainly nothing shocks us more forcibly than this doctrine; and yet, without this mystery, the most incomprehensible of all, we are incomprehensible to ourselves. The knot of our condition receives its turns and convolutions in this abyss, so that man is more inconceivable without this mystery than this mystery is inconceivable to man.

Whence it becomes evident that God, wishing to make the difficulty of our being unintelligible to us by our own efforts, hid the knot of it so high, or rather so low, that we are quite incapable of reaching it. So that it is not by the proud agitations of our reason, but by the single submission of reason, that we can truly know ourselves.

These basic principles, solidly established upon the inviolable authority of religion, reveal to us that there are two truths of faith equally constant: one, that man in the state of creation, or in that of grace, is raised above all nature, made as if like unto God, and sharing in his divinity; the other, that in the state of corruption and sin, he has fallen from that state and been made like the beasts.

These two propositions are equally firm and certain. Scripture declares it to us manifestly when it says in a number of places: "My delights were to be with the children of men" [Proverbs VII, 31]; "I will pour out my spirit upon all flesh" [Joel II, 28]; "You are gods and all of you the sons of the most High" [Psalms LXXXI, 6]; "All flesh is grass" [Isaiah LX, 6]; "Man is compared to senseless beasts, and is become like to them" [Psalms XLVII, 13]; "I said in my heart concerning the sons of man that God would prove them and show them to be like beasts" [Ecclesiastes III, 18]. (434)

184. The last act of reason is to recognize that there are an infinite number of things that are beyond its grasp; it is only weak if it fails to reach the point of recognizing that.

If natural things are beyond its grasp, what will we say of supernatural things? (267)

SECTION B—MOMENTOUS IMPORTANCE OF RELIGION

185. Just imagine a number of men in chains, and all condemned to die, some of whom each day have their throats cut before the eyes of the others. Those who remain see their own condition in that of their fellows and, observing one another with grief and without hope, await their turn. That is the image of the human condition. (199)

186. A man in a cell, not knowing whether sentence has been passed upon him, and having only an hour left to learn it, that hour being sufficient, if he knows that the sentence has been given, for him to have it revoked—it is against nature that he should use that hour, not to inform himself whether the decree has been given, but to play cards. Thus it is not natural that man, etc. . . . . It is a heavy laying on of the hand of God.

Thus, not only the zeal of those who seek him proves God, but the blindness of those who seek him not. (200)

187. Here is an heir who finds the deed to the house he inherits. Will he say, "Perhaps the papers are forgeries," and neglect to examine them? (217)

188. It is ridiculous for us to trust in the company of our fellowmen. Wretched as we, powerless as we, they will not come to our aid; we shall die alone. We must then act as if we were alone; and in that case would we build proud mansions, etc.? We should seek without hesitation the truth; and if we refuse it, we prove thereby that we value more the esteem of men than the search for truth. (211)

189. *Transitoriness*—It is a horrible thing to feel slipping away everything that we possess. (212)

190. Before entering into the proofs of the Christian religion, it seems to me necessary to show the injustice of those men who remain indifferent to seeking the truth of something which is so important to them, and which touches them so closely.

Of all their errors, this is doubtless the one which most clearly proves their folly and blindness, and concerning which it is easiest to demonstrate how much at fault they are through the most obvious observations of common sense and through natural feelings. For it is true beyond all doubt that the time of this life is but an instant, that the state of death is eternal (of whatever nature it may be), and that thus all our actions and thoughts must take such a different course according to the state of that eternity, that it is impossible to take the slightest step with sense and judgment unless one determines it by the consideration of that point which must be our final destination.

There is nothing more obvious than that, and so it is clear that, according to the principles of reason, the conduct of men is quite unreasonable if they do not change their course.

Just consider, then, in this light those who live without thinking of that final goal of life, who let themselves follow their inclinations and their pleasures without reflection and without anxiety, as if they could abolish eternity by turning their thoughts away from it and thinking only of making themselves happy in just this present moment.

And yet that eternity remains, and death, which must admit them to it and which threatens them at every instant, must inevitably place them shortly in the horrible necessity of being eternally either reduced to nothingness or destined to torment, without their knowing which one of these eternities is forever prepared for them.

That is a doubt of a frightful importance. They are in peril of an eternity of torments; and in that situation, as if the matter were not worth the trouble, they do not bother to examine whether these ideas are of the sort that most people accept with a too credulous facility, or of the sort that, though obscure in themselves, have a very solid but hidden foundation. Thus they know not whether there is truth or falsity in the matter, nor whether there is strength or weakness in the proofs. They have those proofs before their eyes, yet they refuse to consider them, and in this ignorance decide to do everything necessary to fall into this misfortune should it exist, to wait until death to put it to the test, to be in the meantime quite content in this state, to declare their satisfaction, and finally to boast of it. Can one think seriously of this matter without being horrified by so unreasonable a behavior?

The tranquil acceptance of this ignorance is a monstrous thing, whose excessive nature and whose stupidity one must make clear to those who spend their life in that state by making them see it clearly in order to overwhelm them by the sight of their own folly. For this is how men reason when they choose to live in this ignorance of what they are, without seeking enlightenment. "I don't know," they say . . . (195)

191. Let them learn at least what the religion is that they are combating before they combat it. If that religion boasted of having a clear view of God and of possessing him clearly revealed and without veils, one might feasibly combat it by saying that one sees nothing in the world which reveals him with that unmistakable clarity. But it says on the contrary that men are in darkness and remote from God, that he has hidden himself from their knowledge as shown by the very name he gives himself in the Scriptures, "a hidden God." [Isaiah XLV, 15] And finally if our religion strives equally to establish these two things: that God has established visible signs in the Church to let those who would sincerely seek him recognize him, and that he has covered them nevertheless in such a way that he may be perceived only by those who seek him with all their heart—then what advantage can they draw when, in their acknowledged neglect of seeking the truth, they cry out that nothing shows it to them, since that darkness in which they find themselves, and which they offer as an objection to the Church, only establishes one of the things the Church itself maintains, without affecting the other, and, far from ruining it, verifies its doctrine?

In order to combat it, they would have to protest that they have made every possible effort to seek the truth everywhere, and even within what the Church proposes, in order to learn about it, but all to no avail. If they spoke thus, they would combat indeed one of its claims. But I hope to show here that there is no reasonable person who can speak in this way, and I venture even to affirm that never has anyone done so. We know quite well how those of this mind act. They think they have made great efforts to inform themselves when they have spent a few hours reading some book of the Scriptures, and when they have questioned a few ecclesiastics about the truths of the faith. Afterwards, they boast that they have vainly sought the truth in books and among men. But, in truth, I shall tell them what I have often said, that this neglect is intolerable. It is not a question here of the slight interest of some outsider, to justify going about things this way. It is a question of ourselves, and of our all.

The immortality of the soul is a thing of such great importance to us, which concerns us so deeply, that one must have lost all feeling to be indifferent about knowing what the truth is in the matter. All our actions and our thoughts must take such different directions depending on whether or not there are eternal goods to hope for, that it is impossible to make a move with good sense and judgment except by determining it by the view of that point which must be our final goal.

Thus our first interest and our first duty is to enlighten ourselves on this subject, upon which all our conduct depends. And that is why, among those who are not convinced of it, I recognize a vast difference between those who strive with all their strength to gain knowledge about it, and those who live without worrying about it and without giving it a thought.

I can have compassion for those who lament sincerely in this doubt, who look upon it as the greatest of misfortunes, and who, sparing nothing in order to escape from it, make of this search their principal and most serious occupation.

But for those who spend their lives without thinking of this ultimate end of life and who, for the simple reason that they do not find within themselves the light that might convince them of it, neglect to seek it elsewhere, and to explore thoroughly whether that opinion is of those that the people accept through a credulous simplicity, or of those that, though obscure in themselves, have nonetheless a very firm and unshakeable foundation, I consider them in quite a different way.

This neglect in a matter that concerns themselves, their eternity, their all, irritates me more than it moves me; it astounds and horrifies me; it is for me a monstrous thing. I do not say this in the pious zeal of a spiritual devotion. I mean on the contrary that one should have this sentiment as a consequence of human interest and an interest of self-love. To that end, one need see only what the least enlightened persons see.

One need not have a very lofty soul to understand that there is in this life no real and solid satisfaction, that all our pleasures are only vanity, that our woes are infinite, and that finally death, which threatens us at every moment, must inevitably place us in but a few years in the horrible necessity of being eternally reduced to nothingness or to a state of misery.

There is nothing more real than that, nor more terrible. Let us put on as bold a front as we will—that is the end that awaits the finest life in this world. Reflect upon it, and then say if it is not beyond doubt that there is no good in this life except in the hope of another life, that one is happy only in proportion as he moves close to it, and that, just as there will be no more woes for those who had a complete assurance of eternity, so there is no happiness for those who remain unenlightened about it.

It is then assuredly a great ill to be in that doubt; but it is at least an indispensable duty to seek, when one is in that doubt. And thus he who doubts and does not seek is at one and the same time both very miserable and very unjust. If he is also tranquil and satisfied, if he professes it and even boasts of it, and if it is even upon this state that he founds his joy and his pride, then I find no term to describe a creature so misguided.

How can one hold such sentiments? What reason for joy can one find in anticipating henceforth only irremediable woes? How can one take pride in seeing oneself in impenetrable darkness, and how is it possible that a reasonable man should reason as follows:

"I do not know who placed me in this world, nor what this world is, nor who I am; I am in a frightful ignorance concerning all things; I know not what my body is, my senses, my soul, and that part of myself that thinks what I am saying, that reflects upon everything and upon itself, and knows itself no more than it knows the rest. I see these terrifying vastnesses of the universe that surrounds me, and I find myself attached to a corner of the vast expanse, without my knowing why I am placed in this spot rather than in another, nor why this brief moment of time that is given to me for my life is assigned to me at this point rather than some other of all the eternity which preceded me and of all the eternity which follows me. I see only infinities on all sides which enclose me as though I were an atom and a shadow that last but one instant without return. All that I know is that I must soon die, but what I am most ignorant of is that very death itself which I cannot escape.

"As I do not know whence I come, so too I know not where I go; and I know only that on leaving this world I fall forever either into the void, or into the hands of an angry God, without knowing which of these conditions is to be eternally my lot. That is my state, full of weakness and incertitude. And from all that, I conclude that I must therefore spend all the days of my life without thinking of what is to happen to me. Perhaps I could find some enlightenment in my doubts, but I do not wish to take the trouble, nor to lift a finger to seek it, and afterwards, treating with contempt those who apply themselves diligently to this undertaking,"—whatever certitude they may have, it is a reason for despair rather than for vanity—"I wish to go, without foresight and without fear; I wish to experience such a great event, and to let myself be led unresisting to death, in uncertainty about the eternity of my future condition."

Who would wish to have for his friend a man who reasons in this way? Who would choose him among others in order to confide in him? Who would have recourse to him in moments of affliction? And finally, what useful rôle could he play in life?

Indeed, it is glorious for religion to have as enemies men so unreasonable, and their opposition to it is so harmless that it serves on the contrary to reinforce the truth of religion. For Christian faith is almost exclusively concerned with establishing these two things: the corruption of nature, and redemption through Jesus Christ. Now I maintain that if they do not serve to show the truth of redemption by the holiness of their lives, at least they serve admirably to demonstrate the corruption of nature by such unnatural sentiments.

Nothing is so important to man as his existence; nothing is so to be dreaded by him as eternity. Therefore, that there should be men indifferent to the loss of their being and to the risk of an eternity of woes is anything but natural. They are quite different concerning all other things: they fear even the slightest things, they foresee them, they feel them, and this same man who spends so many days and nights in rage and despair over the loss of a public position or over some imaginary offense to his honor is the very man who knows that he is going to lose everything by death, without anxiety and without emotion. It is a monstrous thing to see in one heart and at the same time this sensitivity concerning the slightest things, and this strange insensitivity concerning the greatest things. It is an incomprehensible magic spell, and a supernatural trance, which indicates as its cause an almighty force.

A man must have a strangely inverted sense of values to glory in being in such a state, which it seems unbelievable that even one person could endure. And yet experience shows me such persons in so great numbers that it would be surprising if we were not aware that most of those who behave thus are not in reality such as they seem; they are people who have heard that to conform to society's code of manners one should thus act like runaway horses. It is what they call "shaking off the yoke," and this is what they seek to imitate. But it would not be difficult to make them understand how mistaken they are in seeking esteem in this fashion. That is not the way to acquire it, precisely among people of society who are capable of sound judgments and who know that the only way to be successful in seeking esteem is to make themselves appear honest, faithful, judicious, and capable of serving their friends usefully; because men like naturally only what can be useful to them. Now, what advantage is there for us in hearing a man say that he has thus shaken off the yoke, that he does not believe there is a God watching over his actions, that he considers himself as sole master of his own conduct, and that he intends to be accountable to no one but himself? Does he think he has inclined us in this way to have henceforth much confidence in him, and to expect from him consolation, counsel, and assistance in all the emergencies of life? Do such people claim to have caused us to rejoice by telling us that they consider that our soul is only a little wind and smoke, and even by telling us so in a proud and smug tone of voice? Is that really something to be said gaily? Is it not on the contrary something to say sadly, as the saddest thing in the world?

If they thought seriously about it, they would see that their position is so ill-taken, so contrary to good sense, so antisocial, and so remote in all respects from that urbanity which they seek, that they would be more likely to correct than to corrupt those who might have some inclination to follow them. And indeed, just let them set forth their feelings and the reasons they have to doubt religion; they will tell you things so weak and so inconsequential that they will convince you of the contrary. That is what quite appropriately a person said one day to one of them: "If you continue to hold forth in this vein," he said, "in truth you will convert me to Christianity." And he was right, for who would not be horrified to see himself identified with a school of thought in which he would have as companions such wretched persons?

Thus those who profess these sentiments only as a pose would be most unfortunate if they went against their nature to make of themselves the most ill-advised of men. If they regret deep in their heart their lack of faith, let them not hide it; this declaration will be in no wise shameful. There is no shame except in having no shame. Nothing marks more clearly an extreme weakness of mind than not to know what the misfortune of a man without God is; nothing shows more strongly a perverted heart than not to wish the truth of the eternal promises; nothing is more cowardly than boldly to defy God. Let them leave, then, these impieties to those who are sufficiently ill-born to be truly capable of them; let them be at least worthy men if they cannot be Christians; and let them recognize finally that there are two sorts of people who may be called reasonable—either those who serve God with all their hearts because they know him, or those who seek him with all their hearts because they do not know him.

But as for those who live without knowing him and without seeking him, they judge themselves really so unworthy of their own solicitude that they are not worthy of the solicitude of others; and one must have recourse to all the charity of the religion which they disdain in order not to disdain them to the point of abandoning them to their folly. But because this religion obliges us to consider them always, so long as they are in this life, as capable of the grace which may illumine them, and to believe that they may shortly become more filled with faith than we are ourselves, and that we may on the contrary fall into the very blindness which holds them, we must do for them what we should want to be done for us if we were in their place, and summon them to take pity on themselves, and to make at least some effort to see if they will not find the light. Let them devote to reading this a few of those hours which they employ so uselessly elsewhere: no matter what aversion they may bring to it, perhaps they will encounter something in it, and at the worst they will not lose much by it. But to those who will bring to it a perfect sincerity and a true desire to encounter the truth, I hope that they will find satisfaction here, and that they will be persuaded by the proofs of such a divine religion which I have brought together here, and in which I have followed approximately this order . . . (194)

192. [The man Pascal would convert is here speaking.] "This is what I see and what disturbs me. I look in all directions, and I see everywhere only darkness. Nature

offers me nothing which is not a matter of doubt and anxiety. If I saw nothing in it which indicated a Divinity, I should resolve to accept the negative view; if I saw everywhere the marks of a Creator, I should turn to the peace to be found in faith. But seeing too much for me to deny, and too little for me to be sure, I am in a pitiful state. I have wished a hundred times that if a God lies behind nature, it would reveal him unequivocally, and that, if the indications it offers of his existence are deceiving, it would eliminate them completely; that it should say all or nothing, so that I might see what choice I should make. Whereas in the state I am in, not knowing what I am and what I should do, I know neither my condition nor my duty. My heart seeks completely to know where the true good lies so that I may follow it; no price would be too great for me to pay if eternity were to be the reward.

"I envy those whom I see possessing faith and yet living so carelessly, and who employ so ill a gift of which I am sure I would make a quite different use." (229)

SECTION C—CHRISTIAN FAITH AND WHY WE MUST CHOOSE IT

193. "Well then, do you not say yourself that the sky and the birds prove God?"

"No."

"And does your religion not say so?"

"No. For even if that is true in a sense, for a few souls to whom God gives that light, nonetheless it is false so far as the majority are concerned." (244)

194. Nature has perfections, to show that it is the image of God, and faults, to show that it is only his image. (580)

195. *Preface of the second part*—Speak of those who have treated this subject.

I marvel with what rashness these persons undertake to speak of God. Addressing their remarks to nonbelievers, their first chapter is to prove God's existence through the works of nature. I should not be astonished at this undertaking if they were writing for the faithful, for it is certain that those who have a keen faith within their hearts see straightway that everything that is, is nothing other than the handiwork of the God whom they worship. But as for those in whom that light has been extinguished, and in whom one seeks to rekindle it, those persons, bereft of faith and grace and seeking with all their spirit everything in nature which can lead them to that knowledge, find only obscurity and darkness. To tell them that they have only to see the least of the things that lie about them and they will see God made manifest, and to give them for sole proof of this great and important matter the course of the moon and the planets, and to claim to have completed the proof of his existence with such a demonstration, is to give them reason to believe that the proofs of our religion are weak indeed; and I note, by reason and experience, that nothing is more likely to arouse in them disdain for religion.

It is not in this way that the Scriptures, which know better the things which are of God, speak of him. They say on the contrary that God is a hidden God, and that, since the corruption of nature, he has left man in a state of blindness from which he can escape only through Jesus Christ, for except through him all possibility of communication with God has been eliminated: "No one knows the Father but the Son, and he to whom it shall please the Son to reveal him." [Matthew XI, 27]

That is what the Scriptures tell us when in so many places they say that those who seek God find him [Matthew VII, 7]. They are not speaking of a light like that of the sun at noonday. We are not told that they who seek the sun at high noon, or water in the sea, will find them. And thus it must be that God is not evident in nature as they are. And so we are told elsewhere, "Verily, Thou art a hidden God." [Isaiah XLV, 15] (242)

196. But it is impossible that God should ever be the end if he is not the beginning. We direct our vision upward, but we stand upon the sand; and the earth will crumble and we shall fall looking to the sky. (448)

197. Any religion is false which, in its faith, does not worship a God as the beginning of all things and which, in its moral teaching, does not love a single God as the final goal of all things. (487)

198. If there is a single source of everything, a single end of everything, everything must exist by him, everything must exist through him. The true religion must teach us, then, to worship only God and to love only him. But as we find ourselves incapable of worshiping what we do not know, and of loving anything but ourselves, the religion which instructs in these duties must teach us also our incapacities, and must show us also how to overcome them. It teaches us that, through a man, everything was lost, and the tie between God and ourselves broken, and that, through a man, that tie was restored.

We are born so contrary to that love of God, and it is so necessary, that we must be born guilty, or God would be unjust. (489)

199. A mark of the true religion must be that it obliges its followers to love its God. That is very just, and yet none has so ordained except our own. The true religion must also have taken cognizance of our lust and our helplessness; ours has done so. It must have provided remedies to overcome them; one such remedy is prayer. No other religion has asked of God the capacity to love and to follow him. (491)

200. The true religion teaches our duties and our incapacities—pride and lust; and the remedies against them—humility, mortification. (493)

201. Original sin is folly in the eyes of man, but we present it as such. You must not then reproach me with the unreasonableness of this doctrine, since I offer it as being without reason. But this folly is wiser than all the wisdom of men, "For the foolishness of God is wiser than men." [I Corinthians I, 25] For, without it, what can one say of man? His whole state is determined by this imperceptible point. And how could he have perceived it through his reason, since it is a thing contrary to reason, and since his reason, far from inventing it by its means, turns away when it is presented to it. (445)

202. For myself, I confess that as soon as the Christian religion reveals this principle, that the nature of man is corrupt and fallen away from God, it opens our eyes to seeing everywhere the imprint of that truth; for nature is such that it indicates everywhere a lost God, both in man and outside man, and a corrupted nature. (441)

203. Without that divine knowledge, what have men been able to do except either exalt themselves through the inner feeling which they retain of their past greatness, or debase themselves at the sight of their present weakness? For not seeing the whole truth, they have not been able to reach a perfect virtue. Some considering nature as uncorrupted, and the rest as hopeless, they have been unable to avoid either pride or sloth, which are the two sources of all the vices, since they could only abandon themselves to their nature through cowardice, or escape from it through pride. For, if they recognized man's excellence, they were ignorant of his corruption; and thus they avoided sloth but lost themselves in pride. And if they recognized the weakness of man's nature, they were ignorant of its dignity; and thus they could readily avoid vanity, but at the cost of plunging into despair. Thence come the various schools of the stoics and epicureans, the dogmatists and the platonists, etc.

Only the Christian religion has been able to correct these two vices, not by driving out one to replace it by the other, through the wisdom of the world, but by driving out both through the simplicity of the Gospel. For it teaches to the just, whom it raises to the very point of participation in divinity itself, that in this sublime state they bear still the source of all corruption, which makes them, throughout life, subject to error, to misery, to death, to sin; and it cries out to the most impious that they are capable of receiving the grace of their Redeemer. Thus, making tremble those whom it justifies, and consoling those whom it condemns, it tempers fear with hope with so much precision, by virtue of this double capacity for grace and sin which is common to all, that it humbles infinitely more than reason alone can do, but without leading to despair; and it exalts infinitely more than does natural pride, but without presumption. It thus reveals that being alone free of error and vice, it alone can properly instruct and correct men.

Who then can refuse to believe and worship these celestial truths? For is it not clearer than the day that we feel within ourselves the indelible imprint of excellence? And is it not true also that we experience at every moment the effects of our deplorable condition? What, then, if not the truth of these two states, do this chaos and monstrous confusion declare to us, with a voice so powerful that it is impossible to resist? (435)

204. If there were no obscurity, man would not feel his corruption; if there were no light, man would not hope for a remedy. Thus it is not only just, but useful for us, that God should be in part hidden since it is equally dangerous for man to know God without knowing his own wretchedness, and to know his wretchedness without knowing God. (586)

205. Seeing the blindness and the misery of man, looking upon the silent universe and man without light, aban-

doned to his own devices, and as if lost in this little corner of the universe without knowing who put him there, what he has come there to do, what will become of him at death, incapable of any knowledge—I take fright like a man who has been carried in his sleep to a dreadful desert isle and who wakes up not knowing where he is, and with no way of escape. And thereupon I marvel that people are not driven to despair by such a wretched state. I see other persons near me, of a similar nature. I ask them if they are better informed than I, and they tell me no. And then these wretched wanderers, having looked about them, and having seen some attractive objects, have given themselves over to them and become attached to them. As for myself, I could not become attached to them, and considering how probable it is that there is something other than what I see, I have sought whether that God might not have left some mark of himself.

I see several opposing religions, and consequently all false except one. Each wishes to be believed on its own authority, and threatens nonbelievers. I do not believe them, then, when they present themselves that way. Anyone can say that; anyone can declare himself a prophet. But I see the Christian religion in which I find prophesies fulfilled. That is what the others cannot offer. (693)

206. If man is not made for God, why is he happy only in God? If man is made for God, why is he so unlike God? (438)

207. If one does not know himself to be full of pride, ambition, lust, weakness, misery, and injustice, he is very blind. And if, knowing that, he does not wish to be freed of it, what can one say of a man . . . ?

What, then, can one have except esteem for a religion which knows so well man's faults, and what but desire for the truth of a religion which promises such desirable remedies? (450)

208. *Greatness, pettiness*—In proportion as one has more understanding, one discovers more greatness and more baseness in man. As for the common run of men—those who are most lofty, the philosophers, they astonish the common run of men; as for Christians, they astonish the philosophers.

Who will be astonished, then, to see that religion merely knows thoroughly what anyone recognizes in proportion as he gains in understanding? (443)

209. *Infinite—nothing*—Our soul is enclosed within the body, where it finds number, time, dimensions. It reasons about them, and forms thus its concept of nature, of necessity, and cannot believe anything else.

A unit added to infinity in no wise increases it, any more than does the addition of a foot to an infinite measure. The finite disappears in the presence of the infinite, and becomes pure nothingness. So too our mind before God; so too our justice before divine justice. There is no disproportion so great as that between our justice and God's, except the disproportion between a unit and infinity.

God's justice must be enormous like his mercy. Now justice toward the damned is less enormous and must shock less than mercy toward the elect.

We know that there is an infinite, and yet remain ignorant of its nature. Since we know that it is false that numbers are finite, then it is true that there is an infinite in number. But we do not know what it is. It is false that it is even; it is false that it is odd; by adding one, we do not change its nature. Yet it is a number, and every number is either odd or even (it is true that this is understood of every finite number). And so we may well know that there is a God without knowing what he is.

Is there not one underlying truth, seeing so many true things which are not truth itself?

We know then the existence and the nature of the finite, because we are finite ourselves, and have extension. We know the existence of the infinite, and know not its nature, because, while it has extension as we do, it has no limits. But we know neither the existence nor the nature of God, because he has neither extension nor limits.

But through faith, we know his existence; through glory we shall know his nature. Now I have already shown that one can indeed know the existence of a thing without knowing its nature.

Let us speak now according to natural understanding.

If there is a God, he is infinitely incomprehensible since, having neither parts nor limits, he is totally unlike us. We are thus incapable of knowing either what he is, or if he is. That being so, who will dare to undertake to solve this question? Not we, who are of a totally different nature.

Who then will blame Christians for not being able to give a reasonable account of their belief, since they profess a religion for which this is impossible? They declare, in presenting it to the world, that it is a foolish thing; and then you complain that they do not prove it! If they proved it, they would not keep their word; it is by lacking proofs that they are being logically consistent. "Agreed; but even though that excuses those who offer it as such, and frees them from blame for presenting it without reasonable proofs, that does not excuse those who accept it."

Let us examine that point, and let us say, "Either God is, or he is not." But which side shall we favor? Reason can in no way settle the choice; there is an infinite chaos which separates us. A game is being played, at the extremity of that infinite distance, in which either heads or tails will come up. Which will you bet on? By reason, you cannot choose one or the other; by reason, you can defend neither.

Now do not accuse of error those who have made a choice, for you know nothing about it. "No; but I do blame them for making, not that choice, but any choice at all; for, even though he who chooses heads and he who chooses tails are equally wrong, they are both in error. The proper thing is not to bet at all."

That is all very well; but you must bet. There is no

alternative; you are involved. Which will you take, then?
Come now. Since you must make a choice, let us see
which interests you less. You have two things to lose—the
true and the good; and two things to stake—your reason
and your will, your knowledge and your bliss; and your
nature has two things to avoid—error and misery. Your
reason is no more offended by choosing one rather than
the other, since you must necessarily make a choice. That
is one point settled. But your happiness? Let us weigh
what may be gained or lost by wagering that God does
exist. Let us evaluate these two cases: if you win, you win
everything; if you lose, you lose nothing. Wager then without hesitation that he exists.

"All right, then. Yes, I must wager. But perhaps I am
wagering too much."

Let us see. Since the odds of winning or losing are even,
if you had only to win two lives for one, you could still
win. But if there were three to win, you would have to bet
(since you face the necessity of so doing), and you would
be rash, when you are forced to wager, not to risk your life
in order to win three, in a game in which there is an even
chance of winning or losing. But an eternity of life and
happiness is at stake. And that being so, even though there
might be an infinite number of chances, only one of which
would be for you, you would still be right in risking one to
win two; and you will act unreasonably, since you are
obliged to play, to refuse to risk one life against three in a
game in which out of an infinite number of chances there
is one for you, if there were an infinity of infinitely happy
life to be won. But there *is* here an infinity of infinitely
happy life to win, a chance of gain against a finite number
of chances of loss, and what you are staking is finite. That
removes any reason for hesitation. Wherever the infinite is
involved, and there is not an infinite number of chances of
loss against the chance of gain, there is no room to
hesitate, you must give all. And thus when you are forced
to gamble, you must abandon reason if you wish to cling
to your worldly life rather than to risk it for the infinite

gain which is just as likely to occur as the loss of your nothingness.

For it does no good to say that it is uncertain whether you will win; and it is certain that you run a risk; and the infinite distance which exists between the certitude about what you are risking, and the uncertainty about what you may win, balances evenly the finite good that you are certainly risking, against the infinite gain which remains uncertain. This is not so. Indeed, any gambler ventures with certainty in the uncertain hope of winning; and yet he risks the finite with certainty in the uncertain hope of winning the finite, without transgressing against reason. There is not an infinity of distance between this certitude about what what one is risking and the uncertainty of what one may win; that is false. There is, in truth, infinity between the certainty of winning and the certainty of losing. But the uncertainty of winning is in proportion to the certainty of what you are risking, according to the proportion of the chances of winning or losing. And thence it comes that, if there are as many chances on one side as on the other, the odds are even; and then the certainty of what you are staking is equal to the uncertainty of the gain, far indeed from its being infinitely distant. And thus our proposition is infinitely favorable, when you are risking the finite in a game in which there are equal chances of winning or losing, and with infinity to be won. That is perfectly capable of demonstration; and if men are capable of recognizing any truth, this is one.

"I confess it, I admit it. But once more, is there no way of knowing what cards are being dealt?"

Yes. The Scriptures, and the rest, etc.

"Yes, but my hands are tied and my mouth closed. I am being forced to wager, and I am not free; there is no escape for me. And I happen to be so constituted that I cannot believe. What then can you expect me to do?"

That is true. But learn at least that your incapacity to believe, since reason inclines you toward belief and since nonetheless you cannot believe, comes from your passions.

Work, then, not to convince yourself by multiplying proofs of God's existence, but by diminishing your passions. You wish to advance toward faith, and you are ignorant of the road; you wish to recover from your lack of faith, and you seek remedies for it. Learn from people who have been bound like you, and who now stake everything they possess; they are persons who know that road which you would like to follow, and who are cured of an ill you wish to be cured of. Follow the way by which they began; it is by doing everything as if they believed, by taking holy water, by having masses said, etc. Naturally doing those very things will make you believe and will weaken your resistance.

"But that is what I fear."

And why? What have you to lose? . . .

But, in order to show you that that leads to faith, it is certain that that reduces the passions, which are your great obstacles.

End of this discourse—Now what harm will come to you by making this decision? You will be faithful, honest, humble, grateful, kind, a sincere and true friend. In truth, you will not be amid contaminated pleasures, adulated by men, and enjoying physical delights; but will you not have others? I tell you that you will gain by it in this life and that, at each step you take along this road, you will see much certitude of gain, and you will recognize so well the emptiness of what you are risking that you will realize ultimately that you have wagered on something certain and infinite, for which you have given nothing.

"Oh! What you say pleases me, delights me, etc."

If what I say pleases you and seems to you convincing, know that it is said by a man who fell on his knees before and afterwards in order to pray to that Being who is infinite and without parts, to whom he submits all his being, that he might accept submission also of your being, for your own good and for his glory, and that thus strength might be granted to weakness. (233)

210. According to the principle of probabilities, you must take the trouble to seek the truth; for if you die without worshiping the True Cause, you are doomed.

"But," you say, "if he had wanted me to worship him, he would have left me signs of his will."

And so indeed he has done; but you neglect them. Just look for them; that is worth the trouble. (236)

211. *Probabilities*—We must live differently in this world depending upon these contrary suppositions: first, that we could be here forever; second, that it is certain that we shall not be here long, and uncertain that we shall be here even an hour. The latter supposition is the one we must make. (237)

212. If it were wrong to act except when we have certain knowledge, we ought never to do anything concerning religion, for it is not certain. But how many things do we undertake where there is no certainty—sea travel, battles! I say then that upon that principle we ought not to do anything at all, for nothing is certain; and that there is more certainty in religion than there is about our seeing tomorrow, for it is not certain that we shall see tomorrow, but it is certainly possible that we may not see it. You cannot say as much about religion. It is not certain that it is true, but who will venture to say that it is certainly possible that it is not true? Now when we work for tomorrow, and for what is uncertain, we are acting reasonably; for we must work for the uncertain according to the law of probabilities which has already been demonstrated.

Saint Augustine saw that one works for the uncertain at sea, in battle, etc., but he did not recognize the law of probabilities which demonstrates that one must do so. Montaigne saw that we are offended by a distorted mind, and that custom is all-powerful, but he did not see the reason behind these effects.

All these persons have seen the effects, but they have not seen the causes: they are in comparison with those who have discovered causes like those who have eyes only, in comparison with those who have intelligence, for effects are readily visible, and causes are perceptible only to intelligence. And although those effects may be perceived by the intelligence, that intelligence in comparison with the intelligence which perceives causes is like the physical senses in comparison with the mind. (234)

213. *Objection*—Those who hope for their salvation are happy in that hope, but it is counterbalanced by the fear of hell.

Answer—Who has greater reason to fear hell, he who does not know whether there is a hell, and is certain of damnation if there is one, or he who is perfectly convinced there is a hell, and hopeful of being saved if there is? (239)

214. "I should quickly turn away from worldly pleasures," they say, "if I had faith." And I tell you, "You would soon have faith if you had abandoned pleasures." Now it is up to you to begin. If I could, I should give you faith. I cannot do so, nor therefore test the truth of what you say. But you can indeed abandon pleasures, and test whether what I say is true. (240)

215. *Order*—I should be much more afraid of being in error, and finding that the Christian religion was true, than of being in error by believing it true. (241)

216. Faith declares indeed what the senses do not say, but never the contrary of what they perceive. Faith is above, and not against. (265)

217. *Submission*—We must be able to doubt where necessary, to have assurance where necessary, by submitting

where necessary. He who does not act thus does not understand the force of reason. There are some who fail in regard to all three principles, either by their certainty that everything is demonstrable, for lack of understanding what demonstrative proof is; or by doubting everything for lack of knowing where one must submit; or by submitting in all things, for lack of knowing where one must use his own judgment. (268)

218. There is nothing so completely in conformity with reason as this disavowal of reason. (272)

219. How I hate such stupid things as not believing in the Eucharist, etc. If the Gospel is true, if Jesus Christ is God, what difficulty is there in it? (224)

220. It is being superstitious to put one's hopes in rites; but one is guilty of overweening pride in refusing to submit to them. (249)

221. The outward act must be in conformity with the inward disposition if we are to obtain anything from God; that is to say that one must kneel, pray with the lips, etc., so that the pride in man, which was unwilling to submit to God, must now submit to the creature. To expect aid from these outward acts is to be superstitious; to be unwilling to unite them with the inward disposition is to be defiantly proud. (250)

222. For we must not be mistaken about ourselves—we are automatons as much as we are intellectual beings. Thence it comes that the means by which persuasion is effected is not solely logical proof. How few things are actually proved! Proofs convince only the mind. Custom produces our strongest proofs, and the ones most believed. It wins over the automaton in us, and the intelligence is convinced without thinking of it. Who has proved that day

will come tomorrow, and that some time we shall die? And what is more universally believed? It is then custom which convinces us of it. It is custom which makes so many men Christians; custom makes Turks, pagans, artisans, soldiers, etc. (Christians have more than pagans, for they have faith received through baptism.) Finally, we must have recourse to custom when once the mind has discerned where the truth lies so that we may drink deep and steep ourselves in that belief, which eludes us at every moment; for it is much too troublesome to have proofs constantly present in our mind. We must acquire an easier belief, the belief of habit which, without violence, without art, without arguments, leads us to believe things, and inclines all our faculties toward that belief, so that our soul falls naturally into it. When we believe only by the force of conviction, and the automaton in us is inclined to believe the contrary, that is not enough. We must then make both sides of our nature believe: the mind, by reasons, which it suffices to have seen once in our life; and the automaton, through habit, and not by permitting it to yield to the contrary. "Incline my heart into thy testimonies and not to covetousness." [Psalms CXVIII, 36]

Reason acts slowly, and with so many views, on so many principles, which must alway be present, that constantly it grows weary, or wanders, for lack of bringing to bear all its principles. Feeling does not act thus. It acts instantaneously, and always is ready to act. We must then see that our faith becomes a matter of feeling; otherwise it will always be vacillating. (252)

223. Men often mistake their imagination for their heart; and they believe they have been converted as soon as they think of being converted. (275)

224. How great the distance is from knowing God to loving him. (280)

225. Man is not worthy of God, but he is not incapable of being made worthy of him.

It is unfitting for God to join himself to wretched man; but it is not unfitting for God to draw man from his wretched state. (510)

Part III

THE CHRISTIAN LIFE

❧

SECTION A—TRUTHS OF REASON AND OF THE HEART

226. If we submit everything to reason, there will be nothing mysterious and supernatural left in our religion. If we go against the principles of reason, our religion will be absurd and ridiculous. (273)

227. Two excesses: to exclude reason; to admit only reason. (253)

228. It is the heart which feels God, and not the reason. That is what faith is: God perceived by the heart, not by the reason. (278)

229. The heart has its reasons, which the reason does not know; we recognize that in a thousand things. I say that the heart loves the Universal Being naturally, and itself naturally, according to its inclination; and it grows hard toward either one as it chooses. You have rejected one and kept the other. Is it through reason that you love yourself? (277)

230. We know the truth, not only through reason, but also through the heart; it is in this latter fashion that we know first principles, and it is in vain that reason, which has nothing to do with them, seeks to attack them. Skeptics, who devote all their attention to destroying them,

work at it in vain. We know that we are not dreaming; however powerless we may be to prove it by reason, that incapacity reveals only the weakness of our reason, but not the uncertainty of all our knowledge, as the skeptics claim. For the knowledge of first principles, such as the existence of space, time, movement, numbers, is as firm as any knowledge our reasonings give us. And it is on this knowledge of the heart and of instinct that the reason must depend, and it builds on it all its arguments. The heart feels that there are three dimensions in space, and that numbers are infinite; and the reason demonstrates subsequently that there are no two squared numbers of which one is double the other. Principles are felt, propositions are concluded, and all with certitude though by different channels. And it is as useless and as ridiculous for reason to ask of the heart proofs of its first principles before being willing to accept them as it would be ridiculous for the heart to ask of reason an intuition of all the propositions it proves before consenting to admit them.

This powerlessness should then serve only to humble the reason, which would like to judge everything, but not to weaken our certitude, as if only reason were capable of instructing us. Would to God on the contrary that we never had need of reason, and that we knew all things by intuition and feeling! But nature has refused us this gift. She has on the contrary given us only very little knowledge of this sort. All other knowledge can be acquired only by reasoning.

And that is why those to whom God has given religion through the heart's feeling are very happy and quite legitimately convinced. But those who do not have it, we can only give it to them by reasoning until such time as God may grant it to them by the heart's feeling, otherwise faith is merely human and useless for salvation. (282)

231. Faith is a gift of God. Do not get the idea that we are saying that it is a gift of reasoning. Other religions do not say that of theirs; they consider reasoning only a

means for attaining faith, though really it does not lead to it. (279)

232. There are three avenues of belief: reason, custom, inspiration. The Christian religion, which alone has reason, does not recognize as its true children those who believe without inspiration. It is not that it excludes reason and custom, far from it; but one must open his mind to proofs, strengthen his belief by custom, and by humbling himself, prepare to receive inspiration which alone can produce the true and saving effect: "Lest the cross of Christ should be made of no effect." [I Corinthians, I, 17] (245)

233. Instead of complaining because God has hidden himself, you will thank him that he has so freely revealed himself; and you will thank him again that he has not revealed himself to those proud in their learning, for they are unworthy of knowing so holy a God.

Two sorts of people know: those who have a humble heart and who love lowliness, whatever kind of mind they may have, lofty or low; or those who have enough intelligence to recognize the truth, whatever opposition they may feel toward it. (288)

SECTION B—ORIGINAL SIN AND GRACE

234. Their ignorance makes of them blasphemers. The Christian religion consists of two points. It is of equal importance for men to know them, and it is equally dangerous to be ignorant of either. And so it is a consequence of God's mercy that he has given signs of both.

And yet they find a reason for concluding that one of these points does not exist in what ought to have made them conclude the existence of the other. Sages who proclaimed that there was only one God were persecuted, the Jews were hated, and the Christians even more so.

They saw by the light of their natural reason that if there is one true religion on earth the course of all things must direct them toward it as toward their center; the course of all things must have as its goal the establishment and glory of that religion. Men must have in themselves feelings in conformity with its teachings. And, finally, that true religion must be so definitely the goal and center toward which all things gravitate that whoever knows its principles can comprehend fully the nature of man in particular and the course of the world in general.

And on this ground they base their blasphemy against the Christian religion because they know it ill. They imagine that it consists simply in the worship of a God considered as great and powerful and eternal—and that is precisely what deism is, almost as far from Christianity as atheism, which is its exact opposite. And on that score they conclude that this religion is not the true one, because they do not see that all things work together to establish that it is so, and because God does not reveal himself to man with all possible clarity.

Let them conclude from these observations whatever they will against deism; they cannot draw from them any conclusions against the Christian religion which consists essentially in the mystery of the Redeemer who, uniting in himself the two natures, human and divine, has drawn men out of the corruption of sin to reconcile them with God in his divine person.

And so it teaches to men these two truths together: that there is a God whom men can reach, and that there is a corruption in nature which makes them unworthy of him. It is equally important for man to know both these points, and equally dangerous for man to know God without knowing his own wretchedness, or to know his own wretchedness without knowing the Redeemer who can heal him of it. Knowledge of just one of these truths produces the pride of the philosophers who have known God and not their misery, or the despair of the atheists who know their misery but not the Redeemer.

And thus, as it is necessary in equal measure for man to know these two points, so was it necessary that God's mercy let us know them. This is precisely what the Christian religion does; that is its very essence.

Just examine the order of the world in this matter and see whether all things do not tend to the establishment of the two chief principles of this religion: Jesus Christ is the object of everything, and the center toward which everything tends. He who knows that, knows the reason of all things.

Those who go astray do so only for failing to see one of these two things. One can, then, indeed know God without knowing his own wretchedness, and know his own wretchedness without knowing both; but one cannot know Jesus Christ without knowing simultaneously God and one's own misery.

And that is why I shall undertake here to prove by logical reasoning neither the existence of God, nor the Trinity, nor the immortality of the soul, nor any of the things of this sort. Not only should I not feel strong enough to find in nature proofs adequate to convince confirmed atheists, but in any event that knowledge, without Jesus Christ, would be useless and sterile. Though a man should be convinced that numerical proportions are truths immaterial, eternal, and dependent upon a first truth which is their very essence and which is called God, I should not think him because of that recognition very far advanced toward salvation.

The God of the Christians does not consist of a God who is merely the author of geometric truths and of the order of the elements; that suffices only for pagans and epicureans. He is not merely a God who exercises his providence over the life and possessions of men in order to grant a happy succession of years to those who worship him; that suffices for the God of the Jews. But the God of Abraham, the God of Isaac, the God of Jacob, the God of the Christians, is a God of love and consolation; he is a God who fills the soul and heart of those whom he possesses; he is a God who makes them feel inwardly their wretchedness, and his infinite mercy, who joins to him their inmost soul, who fills it with humility, joy, confidence, love; who makes them incapable of seeking anything but himself.

All those who seek God outside of Jesus Christ and who do not go beyond nature, either find no light which satisfies them, or they succeed in forming for themselves a means of knowing and serving God with no mediator between them, and thence they fall either into atheism or into deism which are two things that the Christian religion abhors almost equally.

Without Jesus Christ the world would not continue to exist, for it would have to be destroyed or become a very hell.

If the world existed in order to teach man about God, his divinity would shine out everywhere in it in an incontestable fashion. But as it exists only by Jesus Christ and through Jesus Christ, and to teach men about their corruption and their redemption, proofs of these two truths strike us everywhere.

What appears there reveals neither a total exclusion, nor an obvious presence of the divine, but the presence of a God who conceals himself. Everything bears this stamp.

Shall man who alone knows nature know it only to be wretched? Shall he who alone knows it be in solitary wretchedness? It must not be that he should see nothing at all; but it must not be that he should see so much of it as to believe that he is its master. He must, however, see enough of it to know that he has lost it, for to know what one has lost, one must see and not see, and that is precisely his natural condition.

Whatever choice he makes, I shall not leave him there at rest. (556)

235. *At Port-Royal: beginning, after explaining the incomprehensibility*—The greatness and the miseries of man are so obvious that the true religion must necessarily teach

us both that there is some great principle of greatness in man, and that there is some great principle of misery. It must explain to us these astonishing contradictions.

In order to make man happy, it must show him that there is a God, that he is obliged to love him, that our sole felicity is to be in him, and our sole ill to be separated from him. It must recognize that we are full of darkness which prevents us from knowing and loving him, and that thus our duties obliging us to love God, and our lusts turning us away from him, we are full of injustice. It must explain to us the resistance we have toward God and toward our own good. It must teach us the remedies for these failings, and the way to obtain those remedies. Examine from this point of view all the religions of the world, and see if there is a single one other than Christianity which satisfies these needs.

Will it be the philosophers, who propose to us for sole goods those goods that are within us? Is that the real good? Have they found the remedy to our woes? Is it curing man of presumption to have made him the equal of God? Those who have reduced us to the level of beasts, and the Mohammedans who have given us the pleasures of the earth for sole good, even in eternity, have they found the cure for our lusts? What religion then will teach us to overcome pride and lust? What religion finally will teach us our good, our duties, the weaknesses which turn us away from them, the cause of those weaknesses, the remedies that can correct them, and the means of obtaining those remedies?

All other religions have failed to do so. Let us see what the wisdom of God will do.

"Expect not," it says, "either truth or consolation from men. It is I who have formed you, and who alone can tell you who you are. But you are no longer in the state in which I formed you. I created man holy, innocent, perfect; I filled him with light and intelligence; I communicated to him my glory and my marvels. The eye of man saw then the majesty of God. He was not then in the darkness which blinds him, nor subject to mortality and the sufferings which afflict him. But he could not bear so much glory without falling victim to presumption. He sought to make himself the center of his being, and independent of my help. He slipped away from my domination, and seeking to make himself my equal by his desire to find happiness within himself, I abandoned him to himself, and turning against him the creatures over which he had dominion, I made them his enemies. The result is that today man has become like the beasts, and so far removed from me that scarcely does he retain some confused light concerning his Creator, to such a degree has all his knowledge been wiped out or confused! The senses, independent of reason, and often masters of reason, have led him to the pursuit of pleasures. All creatures either afflict him or tempt him, and dominate over him either by subjugating him by their strength or charming him by their gentleness, which is a more terrible and more imperious domination.

"That is the state in which men are today. They retain some impotent intuition of the happiness of their first nature, and they are plunged into the miseries of their blindness and their lust, which have become their second nature.

"By this principle which I open to you, you can recognize the cause of so many contradictions which have astonished all men, and which have divided them into such diverse schools. Observe now all the impulses of greatness and glory which the ordeal of so many miseries cannot stifle, and see whether it is not necessary that their cause be in another nature."

At Port-Royal, for tomorrow (Prosopopoeia)—"It is in vain, O men, that you seek within yourselves the remedy for your miseries. All your intelligence can only succeed in recognizing that it is not within yourselves that you will find either the truth or the good. Philosophers have so promised you, but they have not been able to bring it about. They know neither what your true good is, nor

what your true state is. How could they have offered remedies for your ills which they have not been able to know?
Your main maladies are pride, which separates you from
God, and lust, which ties you to the earth; and they have
done nothing but encourage at least one of these maladies.
If they have directed your attention to God, it has been
only to develop your pride; they have made you believe
that you were like him and of a similar nature. And those
who recognized the vanity of that claim have cast you into
the opposite pit by persuading you that your nature was
like that of the beasts, and have led you to seek your good
in the satisfaction of the appetites which belong to the
nature of animals. That is not the way to cure you of your
injustices, which these sages have not even recognized. I
alone can tell you who you are . . ."

Adam, Jesus Christ.

If you are united with God, it is through grace, not
because of your nature.

If you are humbled, it is through penitence, not because
of your nature.

Thus, this double capacity . . .

You are not in the state of your creation.

These two states being revealed, it is impossible that
you should not recognize them. Study your impulses, observe yourselves, and see if you do not find within you the
living imprint of these two natures.

Could so many contradictions exist within a single subject?

"Incomprehensible."

All that is incomprehensible exists nonetheless. Infinity
in number, for example. An infinite space equal to a finite.

"But it is unbelievable that God should unite with us."

You draw that conclusion from the spectacle of our baseness. But if you are quite sincere in reaching it, just follow
me a little farther, and recognize that we are indeed so
low that we are by ourselves incapable of knowing
whether God's mercy cannot make us capable of receiving
it. For I should like to know whence this animal, who

recognizes himself so weak, should draw the right to measure God's mercy and to set for it the limits which his fancy suggests to him. He knows so little what God is, that he does not even know what he is himself; and all upset by the spectacle of his own state, he dares affirm that God cannot make him capable of communicating with him.

But I should like to ask him if God expects of him anything more than that he seek to know and love him; I should like to ask him why he believes that God cannot make himself known to him, since man is naturally capable of love and knowledge. It is certain that he knows at least that he exists and that he loves something. Therefore, if he sees something in the darkness which envelops him, and if he finds some object to love among the things of the earth, why, if God reveals to him some ray of his essence, will he not be capable of knowing him and loving him according to the way it shall please him to reveal himself to us? There is without doubt an insufferable presumption in reasonings of this sort, though they seem to be founded on an apparent humility, which is neither sincere nor reasonable if it does not make us confess that, not knowing by ourselves who we are, we can learn it only from God.

[Pascal now imagines God speaking.] "It is not my intent that you should yield your belief to me without reason, and I have no wish to exercise a tyrannical power over you. On the other hand, I do not claim to explain all things to you reasonably. And to reconcile these contradictions, I intend to show you clearly, by convincing evidence, signs of divinity within me that will prove to you what I am, and to establish authority for myself by marvels and proofs which you cannot reject; and I wish then that you will believe the things that I teach you when you find no other reason to reject them except that you cannot yourself know whether they are or are not so."

God has sought to redeem men, and to make salvation accessible to those who will seek it. But men make themselves so unworthy of salvation that it is just that God should refuse to some because of their obduracy what he grants to others with a mercy which they do not merit. Had he wished to overcome the obstinacy of the most obdurate, he could have done so by revealing himself so clearly to them that they could not have doubted the truth of his essence as it will appear upon the last day, with such brilliance of lightning flashes and such convulsions of nature that the dead will rise again and the most blind will see.

It is not in this fashion that he wished to appear, in his advent of mercy; because, so many men persisting in remaining unworthy of his clemency, he wished to leave them suffering the lack of that very good which they refuse. It was not, then, just that he should appear in a manifestly divine fashion, absolutely capable of convincing all men; but it was not just, either, that he should come in so secret a manner that he could not be recognized by those who would seek him sincerely. He sought to make himself perfectly knowable to the latter and thus, wishing to appear openly to those who seek him with all their heart, and to conceal himself from those who flee him with all their heart, he so regulates the degree to which he may be known that he has given visible proofs of himself to those who seek him, and not to those who seek him not. There is enough light for those who wish only to see, and enough obscurity for those of a contrary attitude. (430)

236. It is then true that everything teaches man about his condition, but he must understand it properly, for it is not true that everything reveals God, nor is it true that everything conceals God. But it is true at one and the same time that he hides himself from those who tempt him, and that he reveals himself to those who seek him, because men are at one and the same time unworthy of God and capable of God—unworthy by their corruption, capable by their first nature. (557)

237. If God had never in any way revealed himself, this eternal abstention could be interpreted in two ways, and

might just as well be related to the absence of any divinity as to the unworthiness of men to know him. But because he appears sometimes, and not always, that removes any ambiguity. If he appears once, he *is* eternally; and thus one can only conclude that there is a God and that men are unworthy of him. (559)

238. We conceive neither the glorious state of Adam, nor the nature of his sin, nor the transmission of it even unto us. Those are things which took place in a state of nature totally different from ours, and which exceed the state of our present capacity. We need know nothing of all that in order to escape from our state; and all that it is important for us to know is that we are wretched, corrupt, separated from God, but redeemed by Jesus Christ. Of that we have admirable proofs here on earth. Thus the two proofs of corruption and redemption are drawn from the impious, who live in indifference concerning religion, and from the Jews, who are its irreconcilable enemies. (560)

239. It is true that there is difficulty in entering upon the pious life. But this difficulty does not come from the piety which is beginning to exist within us, but from the impiety which is still there. If our senses were not opposed to penitence, and if our corruption were not opposed to the purity of God, there would be in that nothing difficult for us. We suffer only in proportion as vice, which is natural to us, resists supernatural grace. Our heart feels itself torn between these contrary efforts, but it would be quite unjust to impute this violence to God who is drawing us to him instead of attributing it to the world which is holding us back. It is like a child whom his mother snatches from the hands of thieves; he must love, in the pain he is suffering, the loving and legitimate violence of her who procures his liberty, and detest only the injurious and tyrannical violence of those who are holding him unjustly. The cruelest war which God can bring to men in this life is to leave them without that war which he came

to bring. "Think not that I am come to send peace on earth: I came not to send peace, but a sword." [Matthew X, 34] And further describing the weapons of that war: "I am come to send fire on the earth." [Luke XII, 49] Before him, the world lived in a false peace. (498)

240. There is much difference between tempting and leading into error. God tempts, but he does not lead into error. To tempt is to furnish opportunities without imposing any necessity; if one does not love God, he will then do a certain thing. To lead into error is to place man under the necessity of concluding and following an untruth. (821)

241. Christianity is strange. It orders man to recognize that he is vile, and even abominable, yet orders him to seek to be like God. Without such a counterbalance, that elevation would make him horribly vain, or that humbling would make him terribly abject. (537)

242. The elect will be ignorant of their virtues, and the damned of the greatness of their crimes: "Lord, when did we see you hungry and thirsty . . . ?" [Matthew XXV, 37] (515)

243. All faith consists in Jesus Christ and in Adam; and all morality in lust and in grace. (523)

244. Misery gives rise to despair; pride gives rise to presumption. The Incarnation shows man the greatness of his misery by the greatness of the remedy needed to save him from it. (526)

245. *Lust of the flesh, lust of the eyes, pride, etc.*— There are three orders of things: flesh, mind, will. The carnal are the rich and kings: they are concerned about the body. The seekers after knowledge and the learned:

they are concerned about the mind. The wise: they are concerned about justice.

God must reign over everything, and everything must be considered in relation to him. In matters of the flesh, lust reigns especially; in intellectual matters, desire for knowledge, especially; in wisdom, pride especially. It is not that one cannot be proud about possessions or knowledge, but that is not the usual seat of pride. By granting to a man that he is learned, we do not thereby cease trying to convince him that he is wrong to be proud. The special seat of pride is wisdom, for we cannot recognize that a man has attained wisdom and maintain that he is wrong to be proud, for it is just that he be proud. Thus God alone gives wisdom; and that is why "he that glorieth, may glory in the Lord." [I Corinthians I, 31] (460)

246. To make of a man a saint, grace is absolutely necessary, and anyone who doubts that knows neither what a man is nor what a saint is. (508)

247. If one would declare that man is too insignificant to merit communication with God, he would have to be very great to judge the matter. (511)

248. When we wish to think about God, is there not something which turns us away, tempts us to direct our thoughts elsewhere? All that is evil, and born with us. (478)

SECTION C—THE MYSTERY OF JESUS

249. *Source of contradictions*—A God humiliated even to the point of death upon the cross; a Messiah triumphant over death by his death. Two natures in Jesus Christ, two Advents, two states of the nature of man. (765)

250. *Perpetuity*—Consider that since the beginning of the world the expectation or worship of the Messiah has

continued without interruption; that there were men who proclaimed that God had revealed to them that there was to be born a Redeemer who would save his people; that Abraham came next to say that he had had the revelation that He would be born of him through a son that he would have; that Jacob declared that, from among his twelve children, He would be born of Judah; that Moses and the prophets came afterwards to declare the time and manner of his coming; that they said that the law they possessed was only provisional, awaiting the law of the Messiah; that up to the time of his coming, their law would prevail, but that the other would prevail through all eternity; that thus their law, or that of the Messiah of which it was the promise, would be forever on earth; that indeed it has always endured; that finally Jesus Christ came under all the predicted circumstances. That is admirable. (617)

251. *The Mystery of Jesus*—Jesus suffers in his passion the torments which men inflict upon him; but in agony he suffers the torments which he gives to himself. It is a torment of a hand not human but almighty, and one must be almighty to endure it.

Jesus seeks some consolation at least in his three dearest friends, and they are asleep. He begs them to bear with him for a little, and they leave him with complete negligence, having so little compassion that it could not even prevent them for a moment from sleeping. And thus Jesus was abandoned alone to the wrath of God.

Jesus is alone on earth, with no one feeling and sharing his pain, but with no one knowing it. Heaven and he alone know it.

Jesus is in a garden, not of delights like the first Adam, where the latter worked his ruin and that of the whole human race, but of torments, where He saved himself and the whole human race.

He suffers this sorrow and this solitude in the horror of the night.

I believe that Jesus never complained except on this

single occasion, but then he complained as if he could no longer contain his excessive grief: "My soul is sad even unto death." [Mark XIV, 34]

Jesus seeks companionship and comfort from men. That is unique in all his life, it seems to me. But he receives none, for his disciples are asleep.

Jesus will be in agony until the end of the world. We must not sleep during that time.

Jesus in the midst of this universal abandonment, even by his friends chosen to watch with him and whom he finds asleep, grows vexed because of the peril to which they expose, not him, but themselves, and warns them of their own salvation and their own good with a cordial tenderness for them in spite of their ingratitude, and warns them that the spirit is prompt and the flesh weak.

Jesus prays in his uncertainty concerning the Father's will, and fears death; but, having recognized his will, he goes forth to offer himself to death: "Let us go. He went forth." [Cf. John XVIII, 4]

Jesus addressed an appeal to men, and was not heard.

Jesus, while his disciples slept, effected their salvation. He did it for each of the just while they were asleep, both in their nothingness before their birth, and in their sins after their birth.

He prays only once that the cup pass, and even then with submission, and twice that it come if come it must.

Jesus in lassitude.

Jesus, seeing all his friends asleep and all his enemies vigilant, turns completely to his Father.

Jesus does not consider in Judas his enmity, but the order of God whom he loves, and pays so little attention to his enmity that he calls him friend.

Jesus tears himself away from his disciples to enter into agony; we must tear ourselves away from our nearest and dearest to imitate him.

Jesus being in agony and in the greatest torments, let us pray longer.

We implore God's mercy, not so that he may leave us in

peace in our vices, but so that he may deliver us from them.

If God gave us masters with his own hand, oh how gladly we should obey them! Their necessity and their actions are inevitable.

"Console yourself; you would not seek me if you had not found me.

"I thought of you in my agony; I shed certain drops of blood for you.

"It is tempting me rather than testing yourself to think whether you would do such or such a thing in a certain contingency; I shall do it in you if it arises.

"Let yourself be guided by my rules. See how well I led the Virgin and the saints who let me act in them.

"The Father loves all that I do.

"Do you wish that I should always have to pay with the blood of my humanity, without your shedding any tears?

"Your conversion is my affair; be not afraid, and pray with confidence as for me.

"I am present before you by my word in the Scriptures, by my spirit in the Church and through inspiration, by my power in priests, by my prayers in the faithful.

"Physicians will not heal you, for you will die in the end. But it is I who heal and who make the body immortal.

"Suffer chains, and corporal servitude; at this moment I free you only from spiritual servitude.

"I am to you more a friend than this one or that one, for I have done for you more than they. They would not suffer from you what I have suffered from you, and would not die for you in the time of your infidelities and cruelties, as I have done, and as I am ready to do, and constantly do, in my elect and in the Holy Sacrament.

"If you knew your sins, you would lose heart."

—I must lose heart, then, Lord, for upon your assurance I believe their wickedness.

"No, for I, by whom you learn it, can heal you of them, and what I tell you is a sign that I intend to heal you. In proportion as you expiate them, you will know them, and it will be said unto you, 'See the sins which are forgiven you.' Do penance, then, for your hidden sins and for the hidden wickedness of those you know."

—Lord, I give you everything.

"I love you with an ardor greater than the ardor you have shown in turning to your abominations, 'as a filthy sow to its wallow.' [20]

"Mine be the glory of it, and not yours, worm and earth.

"Reveal to your confessor that my own words are to you a source of evil, vanity, or curiosity."

—I see the depth of my pride, curiosity, and lust. There is no communication between me and God, nor with Jesus Christ in his justice. But through me he assumed sin. All your scourges fell on him. He is more abominable than I; and, far from abhorring me, he is honored that I go to him to succor him. But he has healed himself, and still more so will he heal me. I must add my wounds to his, and join myself to him; and he will save me by saving himself. But I must not add more in the future.

"You shall be as gods, knowing good and evil." [Genesis III, 5] Everyone plays the rôle of God when he passes judgment, saying this is good or bad, and when he is too sore afflicted or rejoices too much over events.

Do small things as though they were great, because of the majesty of Jesus Christ who does them in us and who lives our life; do great things as if they were small and easy because of his almightiness. (553)

252. No other religion has proposed hating oneself. No other religion can then please those who hate themselves and who seek a Being truly worthy of love. And such people, if they had never previously heard of the religion of a humiliated God, would accept it straightway. (468)

253. Not only do we not know God except through Jesus Christ, but we know ourselves only through Jesus

[20] Cf. Horace, *Epistles* I, ii, 26.

Christ. We know life, death, only through Jesus Christ. Outside of Jesus Christ, we do not know what our life is, nor our death, nor God, nor ourselves.

Thus without the Scriptures, which have only Jesus Christ as their object, we know nothing, and see only darkness and confusion in the nature of God and in our own nature. (548)

254. *God through Jesus Christ*—We know God only through Jesus Christ. Without this Mediator, all communication with God is cut off; through Jesus Christ we know God. All those who claimed to know God and to prove him without Jesus Christ had only impotent proofs. But to prove Jesus Christ, we have the prophecies, which are solid and palpable proofs. And these prophecies being fulfilled and proved true by the event, mark the certitude of these truths and, therefore, prove the divinity of Jesus Christ. In him and through him, then, we know God. Otherwise, and without the Scriptures, without original sin, without the necessary Mediator who had been promised and who came, one cannot prove God incontrovertibly, nor teach good doctrine nor good morality. But by and in Jesus Christ one proves God, and one teaches morality and the true doctrine. Jesus Christ is then the real God of men.

But we know at the same time our wretchedness, for that God is indeed he who rescues us from our wretchedness. Thus, we can know God well only by knowing our iniquities. Thus, those who have known God without knowing their wretchedness have not glorified him, but have glorified thereby themselves. "For seeing that in the wisdom of God the world, by wisdom, knew not God, it pleased God, by the foolishness of our preaching, to save them that believe." [I Corinthians I, 21] (547)

255. Consider Jesus Christ in all persons and in ourselves—Jesus Christ as father in his father, Jesus Christ as brother in his brothers, Jesus Christ as poor in the poor,

Jesus Christ as rich in the rich, Jesus Christ as scholar and priest in the priests, Jesus Christ as sovereign in the princes, etc. For he is by his glory everything that is great, being God, and is by his mortal life everything that is weak and abject. For that reason, he took on this wretched condition, to be able to be in all persons, and the model of all conditions. (785)

256. Jesus Christ came to blind those who saw clearly, and to give sight to the blind; to heal the sick, and let the healthy die; to call to penitence and justify sinners, and leave the just in their sins; to fill the poor, and turn the rich empty away. (771)

257. One would have sinned in believing in Jesus Christ had it not been for the miracles. (811)

258. I should not be a Christian were it not for the miracles, said Saint Augustine.[21] (812)

259. Miracles and truth are necessary, because one must convince the whole man, in body and in soul. (806)

260. Miracles prove the power that God has over hearts by the power that he exercises over bodies. (851)

261. "If I had seen a miracle," they say, "I would become a convert." How are they sure that they would do what they know nothing about? They imagine that that conversion consists of a worship of God conducted like the social intercourse and conversations with which they are familiar. True conversion consists in annihilating self before that Universal Being we have so often offended, and who can quite properly destroy us at any moment. It consists in recognizing that we can do nothing without him, and that we have merited nothing from him except his displeasure. It consists in recognizing that there is an in-

[21] In *The City of God* XXII, 9.

vincible opposition between God and ourselves and that, without a mediator, there can be no coming together with him. (470)

SECTION D—THE CHRISTIAN'S FEARS AND JOYS

262. Without Jesus Christ, man must be in vice and misery; with Jesus Christ, man is freed from vice and misery. In him are all our virtue and all our bliss; outside him there are only vice, misery, errors, darkness, death, and despair. (546)

263. The God of the Christians is a God who makes the soul feel that he is its unique good, that all its rest is in him, that it will have no joy except through loving him. He makes it abhor at the same time the obstacles that hold it back and prevent it from loving God with all its strength; self-love and lust, which check it, are unbearable to it. This God makes the soul feel that it has deep within it this self-love which is its ruin, and that he alone can heal it. (544)

264. Self-will will never be satisfied, even though it might be capable of achieving whatever it wills; but one is satisfied as soon as he renounces it. Without it, one cannot be dissatisfied; with it, one cannot be content. (472)

265. There are only two kinds of men: those who are just and think themselves sinners, and the others who are sinners and think themselves just. (534)

266. With how little pride a Christian believes himself united with God! With how little abjection he ranks himself with the earthworms!

This is indeed the way we should accept life and death, goods and ills. (538)

267. What difference is there between a soldier and a Carthusian monk so far as obedience is concerned? Both are equally obedient and dependent, and engaged in equally difficult exercises. But the soldier always hopes to become the master, and never becomes one; for captains, and princes even, are still slaves and dependent. He hopes, however, and keeps working to become the master, whereas the monk takes a vow never to be other than dependent. Thus they do not differ in their perpetual servitude, that both always have, but in the hope that the one has always, and the other never. (539)

268. We owe a deep debt to those who warn us of our faults, for they mortify us. They let us know that we have been despised. They do not prevent our being so in the future, for we have many other faults which merit our being despised; but they prepare the exercise of correction and the elimination of a fault. (835)

269. If it is unnatural blindness to live without seeking what one is, it is a terrible one to live badly while believing in God.

270. Experience makes us see an enormous difference between devoutness and goodness. (496)

271. *Against those who, confident of God's mercy, remain undisturbed without doing good works*—As the two sources of our sins are pride and sloth, God has revealed to us in him two qualities through which to overcome them—his mercy and his justice. The characteristic of justice is to humble pride, however holy the works may be: "And enter not into judgment with thy servant; for in thy sight no man living shall be justified." [Psalms CXLII, 2] The characteristic of mercy is to combat sloth by inviting participation in good works, according to this passage: "God's mercy leads you to repentance" [Romans II, 4]; and this

other of the Ninevites: "Let us do penance to see if perad-venture he will pity us." [Jonas III, 9] And thus, far from mercy authorizing laxity, it is on the contrary the quality which combats it by its very nature. So that instead of saying, "If there were no mercy in God, it would be neces-sary to put forth every effort to attain virtue," we must say on the contrary that it is because there is mercy in God that we must put forth every effort. (497)

272. Let one imagine a body formed of thinking mem-bers. (473)

273. *Members; begin with that idea*—To control the love that one owes to oneself, one must imagine a body formed of thinking members, for we are members of the whole, and see how each member ought to love itself, etc. (474)

274. If the feet and hands had an individual will, never would they perform their proper function except by subor-dinating that individual will to the first will which governs the entire body. Otherwise, they are in disorder and mis-fortune; but, by willing only the good of the body, they achieve their own good. (475)

275. One must love only God and hate only self.
If the foot had remained forever ignorant that it be-longed to the body, and that there was a body on which it was dependent, if it had had only knowledge and love of self, and if it came to know that it belonged to a body on which it was dependent, what regret it would experience, what confusion because of its past life, for having been useless to the body which governed its life, the body which would have reduced it to nothingness if it had re-jected the foot and separated it from itself as the foot had rejected the body. What prayers to be saved! And with what submissiveness it would let itself be governed by the

will which controls the body, even to the point of consenting to be cut off if necessary! Otherwise it would lose its quality as a member, for every member must be quite willing to perish for the body, for which alone everything exists. (476)

276. In order for the members to be happy, they must have a will, and they must make it conform to the will of the body. (480)

277. To be a member is to have no life, being, or movement except through the spirit of the body and for the body.

The separated member, no longer seeing the body of which it is a part, now has only a perishing and dying being. And yet it thinks it is a whole; and, seeing no body on which it depends, it believes it is independent, and wishes to make of itself a center and a body. But having in itself no life principle, it only blunders, and is astonished in the uncertainty of its being, feeling indeed that it is not a body, and yet not seeing that it is a member of a body. Finally, when it comes to know itself, it is as if it had returned home, and it no longer loves itself except for the body. It bemoans its past wanderings.

It could not by its nature love another thing, except for itself and to make it subject to itself, because each thing loves itself more than anything. But in loving the body it loves itself, because it has being only in it, through it, and for it: "But he who is joined to the Lord is one spirit." [I Corinthians VI, 17]

The body loves the hand; and the hand, if it had a will, ought to love itself in the same way as the soul loves it. All love which goes beyond is unjust.

"He who is joined to the Lord is one spirit." One loves himself because he is a member of Jesus Christ. One loves Jesus Christ, because he is the body of which one is a member. All is one, one is in the other, as the three Persons. (483)

278. *Morality*—God having made the heavens and the earth, which do not feel the happiness of their being, he sought to make creatures who would know it, and who would compose a body of thinking members. For our members do not feel the happiness of their union, of their admirable intelligence, of the care that nature takes to make the life principles flow into them, and to make them grow and live. How happy they would be if they felt it, if they perceived it! But for that to be so, they would have to have intelligence to know it, and good will to consent to the will of the universal soul. If, having received intelligence, they used it to retain nourishment in themselves without letting it pass to other members, they would be not only unjust, but miserable also, and would hate themselves rather than love themselves, their happiness, as well as their duty, consisting in consenting to the conduct of the entire soul to which they belong, which loves them better than they love themselves. (482)

279. The true and only virtue is then to hate oneself (for one is hateful by reason of his lust) and to seek a being truly worthy of love in order to love him. But, as we cannot love what is outside us, we must love a being that is in us, and which is not us, and that is true of all men without exception. Now there is only the Universal Being which is such. The kingdom of God is within us, the universal good is within ourselves, and is not ourselves. (485)

280. "For all that is in the world is the concupiscence of the flesh, and the concupiscence of the eyes, and the pride of life." [I John II, 16] Unhappy the cursed earth that these three rivers of fire inflame rather than irrigate! Happy those who, being on these rivers, not plunged into them, not carried along, but immovably firm upon these rivers, not standing, but seated upon a secure and low seat, from which they do not rise until the light, but, after resting in peace, stretch out their hands to Him who is to

raise them up so that they may stand upright and firm beneath the porticos of the holy Jerusalem, where pride will no more attack them and lay them low; and yet they weep, not at seeing carried away all the perishable things that these torrents sweep along, but at the memory of their beloved homeland, of the heavenly Jerusalem, which they recall unceasingly throughout their long exile! (458)

281. The rivers of Babylon flow, and rush downward, and carry away. O holy Zion, where everything is stable and nothing falls!

One must be seated upon the rivers, not beneath or within, but above; and not standing, but sitting, in order to be humble, being seated, and in safety, being above. But we shall be standing beneath the porticos of Jerusalem.

Just examine whether a given pleasure is stable or fleeting; if it passes, it is a river of Babylon. (459)

282. I love all men as my brothers, because they are all redeemed. I love poverty, because he loved it. I love worldly goods, because they make it possible to help the wretched. I keep faith with the whole world. I do not do evil to those who do it to me; but I wish for them a condition like mine in which one receives neither good nor evil from men. I try to be just, true, sincere, and faithful to all men; and I have a tenderness of heart toward those to whom God has joined me most closely; and whether I am alone or before the eyes of men, I know that God sees all my actions, he who must judge them and to whom I have consecrated them all.

Those are my sentiments, and I bless every day of my life my Redeemer who put them in me and who, out of a man full of weaknesses, wretchedness, lust, pride, and ambition, has made a man free from all those ills by the force of his grace to which all glory is due, retaining of myself only the misery and error. (550)

283. There are few true Christians, I maintain, even so far as faith is concerned. There are many who believe, but through superstition. There are many who do not believe, but through their attachment to worldly pleasures. There are few between these two extremes.

I do not include in these categories those who reveal true piety in their lives, and all those who believe through a sentiment of the heart. (256)

284. There is no denying it, one must admit that there is something astonishing about the Christian religion. "It is because you were born a Christian," one may say. Not at all. I am extremely critical, for that very reason, lest that prejudice sway me. But, even though I was born in it, I still find it astonishing. (615)

285. What men by their keenest intellectual efforts had been able to discover, this religion was teaching it already to its children. (444)

286. It is good to be wearied and tired by the vain search for the true good in order to hold out our arms to the Liberator. (422)

287. Only the Christian religion makes man at the same time worthy of love and happy. In social respectability, we cannot be both worthy of love and happy at the same time. (542)

288. The hope that Christians have of possessing an infinite good is mingled with an active enjoyment as well as with fear. Their situation is not like that of those who might hope for a kingdom which in the meantime they could in no degree possess while they are still subjects. Christians hope for holiness and exemption from injustice, and already in some measure they enjoy them. (540)

289. No one is as happy as a true Christian, nor as reasonable, nor as virtuous, nor as worthy of love. (541)

BIBLIOGRAPHY

❧

FRENCH EDITIONS
OF THE WORKS OF PASCAL

Œuvres complètes, publiées par Brunschvicq, Boutroux, et Gazier, 14 vols. (Paris, 1904-1925).
Œuvres complètes, publiées par Fortunat Strowski, 3 vols. (Paris, 1923-1931).
Œuvres complètes, texte établi par Jacques Chevalier (Paris, 1954).

ENGLISH EDITIONS

The Living Thoughts of Pascal, presented by François Mauriac (New York, 1940).
Pascal's Pensées, bilingual edition, trans. R. F. Stewart (New York, 1950).
Pascal's Pensées, trans. Martin Turnell (New York, 1962).

FRENCH STUDIES

Béguin, Albert, *Pascal par lui-même* (Paris, 1952).
Brunschvicq, Léon, *Pascal* (Paris, 1932).
Chinard, Gilbert, *En lisant Pascal* (Paris, 1948).
Cresson, André, *Pascal, sa vie et son oeuvre* (Paris, 1962).
Demorest, J., *Pascal écrivain* (Paris, 1957).
Lafuma, Louis, *Histoire des Pensées de Pascal* (Paris, 1957).
Mesnard, Jean, *Pascal, l'homme et l'oeuvre* (Paris, 1951).
Strowski, Fortunat, *Pascal et son temps* (Paris, 1907).

ENGLISH STUDIES

Bishop, Morris G., *Pascal* (New York, 1936).

Cailliet, Emile, *Pascal: the emergence of genius* (New York, 1961).

Mesnard, Jean, *Pascal, his life and works* (New York, 1953).

Mortimer, E., *Blaise Pascal* (New York, 1959).

Roberts, James D., *Faith and Reason: a comparative study of Pascal, Bergson, and James* (Boston, 1962).